creating a
beautiful little

Christmas

Teri Ahlm
from
A BEAUTIFUL LITTLE LIFE

creating a
beautiful little
Christmas

Table of Contents:

To the Reader:

Bigger isn't always better...especially when it comes to celebrating the holidays. "Creating A Beautiful Little Christmas" will help you determine what's important to you during the holidays, and help you to create a meaningful celebration that you enjoy.

This book contains hundreds of ideas to help you create a beautiful Christmas for you and your family:

- Decorate your home inside and out beautifully, inexpensively and without stressing out.
- Look your best all season long by adding a little sparkle and shine to your wardrobe basics.
- Pledge to take care of yourself and make time to nurture your spirit during this busy time of year.
- Find meaning in the season, even if you're not religious.
- Perfect the art of gift giving for everyone on your list.
- Entertain your guests without breaking a sweat by planning ahead.

By keeping things small, you'll soon see that you have more time available for the things that are really important to you. When your holidays are filled with things that are meaningful to you, you are "Creating A Beautiful Little Christmas."

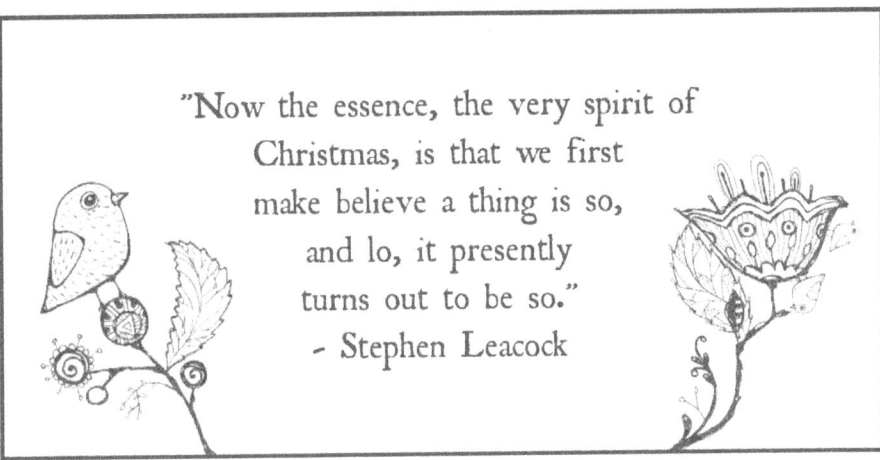

"Now the essence, the very spirit of
Christmas, is that we first
make believe a thing is so,
and lo, it presently
turns out to be so."
- Stephen Leacock

Chapter 1
Your Ideal Christmas

A friend told me recently that he wished he could skip the entire month of December and just skip from Thanksgiving to the New Year.

He went on to explain that, to him, the holidays were just a drain. He always ended up feeling let down when it was all said and done, and the whole season was just exhausting.

I think that many of us dread the holidays, or at least parts of the season. We all have high expectations when it comes to celebrating Christmas. After all, it's supposed to be a magical time of year, right? The reality is that it's those high expectations that can lead to disappointment and can make the season an incredibly stressful, financially draining, and completely overwhelming time of year.

What would it take for Christmas to actually be the magical time that we think it should be? Is it really possible to create a beautiful Christmas by scaling back?

The Ghost of Christmas Past

As a child, Christmas was the most exciting time of year. I remember counting down the days until Christmas Eve, and hardly sleeping a wink waiting for Santa. These magical memories will be with me forever, but that doesn't mean that Christmas is the same when you are an adult.

As a child we had no idea if Uncle Jim had too much to drink, if mom maxed her credit account on gifts, or if the tree was lopsided. All we remember is the magic of waking up on Christmas morning with gifts under the tree, a Christmas feast later in the day and lots of friends and family around.

The reality is that as adults, we have a whole different perspective on the holidays. We DO notice if someone drinks too much or acts inappropriately. Budgeting carefully to be able to get the best gifts under the non-lopsided tree is basically our job, and we have to prepare the feast for all of the friends and family.

What I'm trying to say is that those fairy-tale Christmas memories we have aren't real. It's not possible for us to have a holiday like the ones that we remember from our childhood. As adults, we carry the responsibility of providing that sort of holiday magic for our friends and family.

What's In Your Way

We can't go back in time to when we were kids at Christmas time, but we can make this Christmas special for not only those around us, but for ourselves as well. We can add meaningful touches to the mundane tasks that we do to show our love to our friends and family. We can create an environment in our home that is warm, comfortable and nurturing so that everyone can relax and enjoy themselves. We can entertain with grace so that nobody feels left out or put out!

In order to do all of these things, we need to remove some of the baggage that's in our way; the expectations that we have that are unrealistic. We all have them!

Kids who argue and fight all year are not going to stop just because it's Christmas. As a matter of fact, they may fight more if they pick up on tension and stress coming from you. Expecting your significant other to decorate the Christmas tree with you when you know that he/she hates decorating is setting yourself up for conflict, and there's no quicker way to ruin your peaceful holiday dream!

Let's get real.

Making It Real

Knowing and understanding in advance what you're getting into is key to creating a beautiful little Christmas for you and your family. The kids are going to fight. If "Santa is watching!" doesn't work, you'll need to have a few tricks up your sleeve to distract them. A friend or family member who loves decorating would probably love an invitation to help you with your tree as much as your significant other would love NOT decorating.

The chores, the projects, the decorating, the cooking and cleaning, the wrapping of the gifts, the baking, the shopping – those ARE the joys. Those are the things that make Christmastime beautiful and create special memories for you and yours.

The holiday season will only be as great as the amount of effort you put into making it a great holiday season. Let me say that again...

 "The holiday season will only be as great as the amount of effort you put into making it a great season."

If you don't take time to do projects, start new family traditions, cook and bake, etc. you won't find much joy in the holidays. The key to creating a beautiful little Christmas lies in the word <u>little</u>. Small things done with great love mean SO much more than shallow, over the top gestures.

Getting caught up in creating an extravagant Christmas with perfection in every detail is not going to bring you nearly as much joy as creating a few simple traditions that leave you with more time to spend with your family and friends.

It seems to me that no matter how hard I try, there's always SOMETHING that doesn't come out right. When things go wrong, and you know they will, having a sense of humor can go a long way to making a Christmas memory that is pleasant instead of tragic.

One of my favorite movies to watch at Christmastime is "A Christmas Story." I love the part when the "bumpus dogs" eat the turkey that is to be their Christmas feast, so the family ends up having their Christmas dinner at a Chinese restaurant. Are they upset when it happens? Of course. But the laughter and love shared by the family during their Chinese Christmas dinner is absolutely what Christmas should be about!

As you go through the rest of this book, do it with the idea that some of the things that you plan on aren't going to turn out exactly how you want them to... and that's okay. The end result may not be what you expected, but that doesn't mean that it won't be a beautiful finish.

 "Christmas doesn't have to perfect to be beautiful."

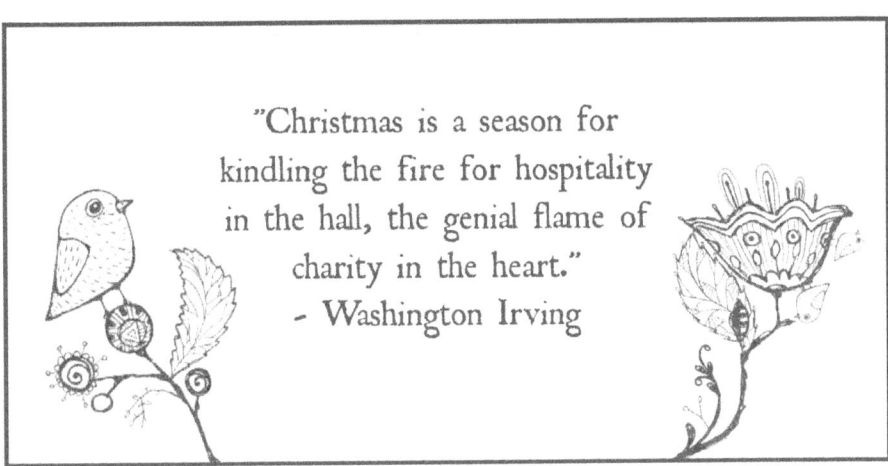

"Christmas is a season for
kindling the fire for hospitality
in the hall, the genial flame of
charity in the heart."
- Washington Irving

Chapter 2
Simply Beautiful Holiday Decor

Going all out when it comes to decorating for the holidays seems to
be the norm these days. A decorated Christmas tree for each floor
of the home, (or for each ROOM) evergreen swags over the
doorways, and candles aglow. Outdoors there are trees lit with
blinking multicolored bulbs, giant, inflatable snowmen, reindeer,
and a sleigh.

I can't imagine the work that decorating your home to that extent,
both inside and out, entails. Not only do you have the expense of
purchasing the decorations initially, but you have to haul them out
of storage, set everything up for the season, and then after just a
short season you have to take it all down, pack it up, and put it back
into storage.

The thought of decorating this way is completely overwhelming to me. I actually believe that all of that work and all of that "stuff" takes away from rather than adds to the beauty of the season. By scaling back on holiday decorating, you free up time in your schedule to spend with your family, do a little shopping, or just relax and enjoy some time alone!

Decorating for the Season

That doesn't mean that your home has to remain undecorated for the holidays. I like to simplify my holiday decorating by using more seasonal items and fewer holiday themed items. By decorating my home for the winter season instead of the Christmas holiday, I'm creating a warm, cozy atmosphere that will last from the day after Halloween to just before Easter.

Simplify holiday decorating by using more **seasonal** items and fewer **holiday** themed items.

There are many ways that you can decorate for the winter season and at the same time, add warmth to your home for the holidays:

- Use a large, decorative, basket, bucket, or bin for firewood or kindling next to the fireplace. If you don't have a fireplace, fill your basket with throw blankets, books, or pine boughs.

- Add some warm, cozy throw blankets and soft, fluffy pillows throughout your home. Furry skins (real or faux) are EVERYWHERE right now.

- Candles create instant warmth and are an inexpensive way to decorate for the season. If you have pets, consider battery operated wax candles. Many can be set to turn on and off automatically every day. I absolutely love them!

- Bringing a bit of the outside in is a beautiful way to accent your tables, trays and mantle. Pine boughs and pine cones, rustic wood, nuts, and berries are great.

- Area rugs not only warm up the floors literally, but a patterned area rug can make a room feel warmer, too.

- Think outside the box. Using a plaid blanket as a tablecloth is a fun, casual look. An inexpensive rug adds a cozy touch to the back of a chair.

- In your living room, move your furniture away from the walls and create an intimate conversation area.

- Decorate with warm colors: Golds, oranges, and reds instantly cozy up a room. Just adding a few accessories in warm tones can make a big difference.

- Try warming up your overall atmosphere with scent. Lavender and vanilla are calming, citrus scents help give you energy, and of course pine and cinnamon are festive.

- To me, a house without books isn't a home. Coffee table books, books on current interests, even magazines can give guests a break from the stress of the holidays.

What Does Your Christmas Look Like?

So many of us have an accumulation of hand-me-down decorations that we use each year. Some of mine are end of the year clearance items, some are inherited ornaments, and most of them don't really reflect the way that I see the holidays. For the last several years many of the decorations that I have didn't get unpacked at all.

I'm not saying that you should go out and buy all new holiday decor, but instead keep things simple. Think about how you'd like your home to look over the holidays. Instead of putting out the same collection of items this year, why not choose just 2 colors of decorations to put out? Using only blue and silver ornaments is beautiful. Gold with all white or with jewel toned ornaments looks much more sophisticated than a multicolored jumble and is so much easier!

For a sophisticated look, pick just two colors of decorations to use this year. A jewel tone with a neutral is super hot!

Be selective and decide in advance which items are important to you when it comes to your holiday decor. For me, it's important that we have a real Christmas tree in the house. It doesn't need to be a big tree, but I love the smell of a real Christmas tree. To me, the tree is the center of my holiday decorating and everything else is kept quite simple.

The goal is to change things up. Just because you have a box of ornaments that you hang on your artificial tree each year doesn't mean that you can't do it different this year. Again, it's not about shopping for all new decorations. It's about being a bit more selective about what you use and putting the carefully chosen items that you'll use where you'll be sure to see them often and they will bring you the most joy.

 Check "Creating A Beautiful Little Christmas" on Pinterest for tons of decorating inspiration! www.pinterest.com/LittleXMas/

Look Festive Without Going Overboard

When you select your favorite items and are thoughtful about where you place them, there is no danger of going overboard with your holiday decorating. Maybe, like me, your focus is on the tree, and that is where you spend most of your time and attention. Maybe you have one of those villages of ceramic houses and you find great pleasure in setting it up each year. Whatever your thing is, pick one focal point of decor and make it absolutely breathtaking. That one focal point, combined with your seasonal decorations that make your home cozy and warm, create an atmosphere that is festive without being overdone!

The Tree & Tree Alternatives

As I mentioned, having a real Christmas tree is important to me, but this year, for many reasons, we are planning on getting a smaller tree. First, we have a puppy and I can't imagine what she would do with a tree on the floor in the living room! Second, it won't take up as much room. Finally, because I've never liked a frilly tree skirt, I'll be looking for a tree that is small enough to be in a pot or basket.

If you don't want a real tree, there are a ton of alternatives to the traditional Christmas tree. Surprisingly enough, a branch in a large vase with a few small ornaments can be quite lovely, and there are a million do-it-yourself ways to create a "tree" out of driftwood, pine boughs, even vintage brooches!

Whatever your plans are for this Christmas, keeping the decor simple and beautiful will free up more time for you and help you focus on creating a beautiful little Christmas for you and your family.

"Christmas waves a magic wand over this world, and behold, everything is softer and more beautiful."
- Norman Vincent Peale

Chapter 3

Your Holiday Style

Every year is the same. The holiday season rolls around, the invitations start coming in, and I start to panic about having nothing to wear. There are gatherings with co-workers, friends, family - and they all require something special to wear!

Putting together a festive look is actually quite simple once you figure out the formula. All it takes is adding a little SPARKLE and SHINE!

Why How You Look Matters

Fashion is about more than wearing the latest trends. It's about feeling great because you know that you look your best. It's about looking good on the outside to reflect how you feel about yourself on the inside.

Choosing to dress yourself in clothes that you love and help you to feel your best is a very special gift that women can give themselves.

It doesn't have to cost a lot of money to find nice things, but it does take time and effort! Taking that time in the morning to make a careful selection of what you wear can make a huge difference in the way that you feel all day long. During the holidays, it's more important than any other time of the year to have a few great outfits that you can throw on any time and know that you look absolutely great.

Festive Casual Style

Festive casual style is just exactly what it sounds like. Sometimes you need to dress to the nines for a special event during the holiday season, but for the most part you don't need cocktail attire. When you're working, shopping, entertaining or running errands, what you really want is a casual look with a touch of something special to make it more festive.

One easy trick is to start with a single color outfit. Monochromatic dressing not only helps you look thinner, it also adds just a bit of sophistication.

Those white jeans in your closet that you rocked all summer? Pair them with a white silk top or a luxe fisherman's sweater for a head to toe white look that is stylish and festive. Don't worry if your whites don't match – they don't have to!

 Black jeans and a black turtleneck are a perfect holiday uniform for running errands. Add a few accessories and you'll look great on the go!

A pair of black leggings, jeans, or cropped black pants with a black sweater or a tunic is a fabulous base to start building a special outfit.

And don't be afraid to start with a head to toe outfit in a bright color. Those plum skinny jeans from last winter with a tee or sweater in a similar hue are perfect for creating the kind of look you're after.

Putting together a monochromatic look is incredibly easy. So easy that you don't even have to think about it for more than one second. That's why it's my go-to way to dress when I'm busy or under stress.

Once you have the basic monochromatic outfit, all you need to do is add a bit of sparkle and shine. It's easy to do with a few inexpensive accessories.

Adding Sparkle & Shine

LAYER 1: DRESS UP YOUR NECKLINE

Add a bright scarf in an animal print or a soft floral. Or consider a statement necklace with some real bling. A collar peeking out from under your shirt is another way to dress up your neckline.

LAYER 2: DRESS UP YOUR FEET

Cool, comfortable footwear will make your monochromatic outfit fab! Adding a pair of biker boots, wedge booties, dressy pumps, colorful flats or print sneakers will really give you a chance to show some personality.

LAYER 3: PULL IT TOGETHER

Throw on a denim jacket if it's chilly outside or a classic trench for a more sophisticated look. A sparkling cardigan or velvet blazer are perfect for parties, and you can throw on a chambray shirt for baking.

LAYER 4: IT'S IN THE BAG

Grab your choice of handbag and you are good to go. Whether it's a large hobo bag, a small clutch or something in between have fun with your choice!

Making It Work

A plaid cashmere scarf and a pair of riding boots with the black leggings and tunic are easy, totally comfortable, and very trendy. Plaid is still incredibly hot this season as the 90's "grunge" style comes back in full force. Don't go overboard with plaid – a few pieces go a long way – but when you throw on a jacket and grab a casual bag you have a complete look that will take you anywhere.

Statement necklaces are also still really hot and they can make a white sweater and jeans look brilliant for happy hour! You can find gorgeous statement necklaces for under $25 that make any simple outfit special enough for a party!

A statement necklace gives you instant sparkle. www.chicnova.com has them for under $10 - and they make a great gift!

Certain styles of tops don't fit well with a large necklace. In that situation, you can substitute that statement necklace with a great pair of chandelier earrings, a stack of bangle bracelets, or a bright colored belt.

A vintage handbag, a funky pair of shoes or a beautiful scarf can be a perfect way to break up a monochrome outfit, too.

When you start with the blank canvas of a head to toe monochromatic outfit, you can add any combination of items in layers 1 through 4 and not have to worry in the least if it matches, if it looks pulled together, or if you are dressed appropriately. You can be confident that you look stylish and classy!

The Black Skirt

You absolutely can't go wrong with a black skirt at Christmastime. A black skirt with black tights can be dressed down with a denim shirt and boots OR dressed up with heels and a sequined top.

Skater skirts are all the rage this year, but to me they seem really young. A classic pencil skirt is universally flattering and always in style! If you prefer a little more fullness, you could opt for a midi – a mid-length skirt with a gathered waist.

 "Three Black Skirts" is a great book by Anna Johnson. It came out in 2000, but it's still true. "Three Black Skirts" **is** all you need to survive!

If you have a slim fitting skirt, like a pencil skirt, you can wear a top with more fullness. A close-fitting leather shirt with a full, peplum waist would be beautiful, but you could also pair it with an oversized cable knit sweater.

A full skirt looks best with a lightweight, close-fitting sweater or tee. A rich, jewel-toned turtleneck (another classic that's red hot this year!) would be perfect!

Layer it on!

Here in Minnesota it's COLD during November and December. You're outdoors, in a cold car, dealing with snow and ice, then minutes later, you're inside with a fire in the fireplace and 50 people in a living room!

What's the best way to cope? Dress in layers! There are a few things to keep in mind to keep your layers from looking too bulky... The last thing any of us want is to look bigger!

Start with a whisper thin turtleneck as a base layer. Just make sure it's not so thin that you can see through it. (Unless that's the look you're going for!) You'll be wearing it alone for most of the festivities!

A white button-down is another versatile first layer, and odds are that you already have one in your closet. Tuck it in, or leave it out, whichever you prefer.

 Dressing in layers is the key to comfort during holiday parties. Just make sure they are lightweight so you don't add bulk!

Add a cardigan or a chunky knit sweater for your next layer. It will give lots of warmth AND give a nice contrast to the crispness of the turtleneck or white button-down underneath. Let the hem of the base layer peek out at the bottom for a little extra interest.

A beautiful coat tops things off with a super-warm layer that can be shed the minute you walk in the door. There are as many options as you can imagine for coats. Just make sure that, again, you're not adding too much bulk. This might not be the time to break out the down-filled parka!

If you're using bold colors or patterns in your layered look, make sure that you put darker shades under the lighter ones to keep the proportions looking right.

One last thing: Make sure that your clothes are all in good repair and fit you properly. Distressed denim is one thing, but if your clothes look shabby you won't look good no matter what!

 # *do:*

Before you walk out the door,
CHECK YOURSELF!

Make sure that your sweater is free of
pulls, pills, or snags.

Check your jeans, tights or leggings for
saggy tush or knees.

Are your boots or shoes scuffed? Do they
have salt stains?

CHECK YOUR REAR VIEW! Walk around
your house for a few minutes and then
check again. If your skirt rides up, make
sure your bits and pieces aren't showing!

don't:

I don't care if your yoga pants cost more
than my whole outfit! They are not
appropriate for you to wear to a party.

Leggings are not pants. If you wear them
outside the house, make sure that your
bottom is covered.

"I will honor Christmas in my
heart, and try to keep it all
the year."
- Charles Dickens

Chapter 4
Easy Entertaining

Entertaining a crowd during the holidays doesn't have to interfere with your enjoyment of the celebration. It's easy to allow the cooking and cleaning to overwhelm you. One thing leads to another and the next thing you know you've added side dishes, invited " just a few" more guests, shopping for a last minute replacement for the area rug with that stain, decorating just a little bit more, and fretting about not having dishes with little Christmas trees on them. The next thing you know, you're in over your head and definitely NOT enjoying A Beautiful Little Christmas!

Stop the Insanity!

When I prepare our holiday dinner, I'm now cooking for just 4 people. It feels a little odd to have such a small celebration after growing up in a family of 13 (yes, 11 kids + mom and dad) that all got together over the holidays. For me to prepare a feast even close to the same as my mother prepared would be absurd! She would make both ham and turkey, stuffing, potatoes, green bean casserole, some sort of noodle hotdish, salads, and I can't even remember what else. There were dinner rolls, poppyseed rolls, cakes, pies, and cookies enough to make your head spin! I don't know how she did it, and I'm thankful that I don't have to prepare dinner for that many people. That said, it's hard to not compare my holiday meal to those that my mom prepared decades ago.

In this house, we aren't a formal kind of family, so a fancy dinner doesn't happen very often, but I do I enjoy the planning, prepping and cooking of a delicious meal!

A little planning goes a long way to making your time in the kitchen easier. Plan your menu, write it down, and stick to it!

For me, the key is in the planning. A little planning can mean the difference between being able to spend time with the family after opening gifts on Christmas morning and missing it all because I'm in the kitchen.

Don't worry, when I talk about planning I'm not talking about checklists, binders full of worksheets or calendars counting down your tasks. That kind of planning, to me, makes things more complicated instead of simpler! I'm talking about simple things that you can do to make things easier for yourself.

Make Ahead Meals

When I'm planning for and shopping for the ingredients for baking and for the holiday meals that I'll prepare, it never fails. Every year, I get a plan and then I realize that I have forgotten to shop for any food for us to eat in the few days just before Christmas!

It's easy to focus on Christmas dinner and lose sight of all of the daily meals that still need to be prepared. Instead of eating takeout for a week before Christmas, this year plan ahead! You can start making a few meals now to freeze that you can pop in the oven or crock pot on your busiest days. It's easy! When you're cooking dinner, double the batch and freeze half of the dish for later!

I'm including a few of our favorite recipes for you. They aren't gourmet, (by any means) and they may not be extremely healthy, but they ARE easy, they freeze well, and they'll help make things much easier for you as the holidays approach.

Super Simple Beef Tips

1-2 lbs cubed beef
1 pkg fresh mushrooms (if desired)
1 package dried onion soup mix
1 package dried beef gravy mix
1 can cream of mushroom soup
1 c water

Combine dried onion soup mix, dried gravy mix, cream of mushroom soup and water. Mix well and pour over cubed beef in your crock pot or in a casserole pan.

Add fresh mushrooms and stir to coat.

If using the crock pot, cook on low for about 5 hours. If baking in the oven, cover your casserole tightly with foil and bake for 3 hours at 300°.

Serve over mashed potatoes, rice or pasta.

Easy Chicken Marsala

4 boneless, skinless chicken breasts
salt & freshly ground black pepper
1/2 c all purpose flour
2 Tbsp olive oil
1 package fresh mushrooms
2 Tbsp butter
1/2 c sweet Marsala wine
1/4 c chicken stock
1/4 c sherry or dry white wine
2 Tbsp heavy cream

Pound chicken breasts with a meat tenderizer until they are about 1/4" thick. Salt and pepper well, then dredge in flour.

Heat olive oil in frying pan and fry each piece of chicken for about 3-4 minutes per side or until golden brown. Set aside chicken, covering to keep warm.

Saute fresh mushrooms in butter for 4-5 minutes. Add Marsala wine, chicken stock, sherry or dry white wine, and cream. Simmer about 3 minutes. Pour over chicken and serve.

Loaded Baked Potato Casserole

2 lbs chicken breasts,
  cubed or shredded
10-12 small red potatoes, diced
1/2 c olive oil
1 tsp salt
1 Tbsp freshly ground black pepper
1/2 Tbsp garlic powder
2 c Mexican blend cheese
1/2 c bacon, crumbled
1/2 c chopped green onion

Preheat oven to 475°. Mix oil, salt, pepper, & garlic powder. Add potatoes & coat well. Place into a greased baking dish, reserving seasoning mixture. Bake 1 hour, stirring every 20 minutes.

While potatoes are baking, coat chicken with seasoning mixture. Cook in skillet over medium heat until no longer pink.

When potatoes are finished baking, turn oven temperature down to 400°. Add the chicken, cheese, bacon & green onion to the baking dish.

Bake 5 minutes or until cheese is melted. Serve with sour cream or ranch dressing.

Chicken & Stuffing Casserole

4 large chicken breasts,
  cooked and shredded
2-1/2 c chicken broth
2 cans cream of chicken soup
2 boxes stove top stuffing
1/2 c butter

Preheat oven to 350°. Place the shredded chicken in the bottom of a casserole pan – approximately 9x13.

Spread both cans of soup over the chicken, then sprinkle the stuffing over the soup. Pour the chicken broth and melted butter over the stuffing.

Bake for 1 hour or until stuffing is golden brown.

Beef Pasty

1 small pie crust per pasty
1-1/4 lbs beef, diced
2 small onions, diced small
1 potato diced in 1/4" pieces
1 small rutabaga, cut in 1/4" pieces
2 tsp salt
1 tsp freshly ground black pepper

Precook the beef, braising in a warm oven for 2 hours.

Dice the onion, potatoes and rutabaga. Dice the cooked beef. Combine in a large mixing bowl and season with salt and pepper. Allow to cool.

Using 1 c of filling per pie crust, place filling in middle, then fold over and crimp edges to create a hand pie. At this point, these can be tightly wrapped and frozen for weeks!

When ready to serve, cook in a 425° oven for 30 minutes - 1 hour if frozen. Serve with gravy or ketchup.

 These simple meals also make great gifts for elderly neighbors, new parents, and busy friends. Prepare them in a foil pan, put a piece of pretty paper on the lid with cooking instructions, and tie it all up with a bow.

Simple Menu Plans

When it comes to the holiday feast, there are 5 key components that are essential to a classic Christmas dinner:

1. Starters & Beverages

2. Sides

3. Main Dishes

4. Desserts

5. Extras (breads, muffins, rolls)

Within each category, you can be as simple or elaborate as you choose, but by making sure that you have all 5 of the key components covered, you can be sure that your meal will be a hit.

 If you go all out on the main course, it's ok to keep your sides and dessert simple. It's all about BALANCE!

I think that if you go all out on one category, you can take some shortcuts on the rest. If appetizers are your thing, then go all out and make several delicious, gourmet appetizers and keep the main dish and sides simple. If your priority is that the main dish be absolutely perfect, then purchase frozen appetizers that just need to be reheated and rolls from your local bakery. It's all about balance!

My favorite dinner to serve on Christmas eve is beef tenderloin Bearnaise, garlic butter shrimp, baked potatoes, and a big green salad. We usually start with a cheese tray, crackers and fruit, some hummus and vegetables, and some chips. I'll open a bottle of wine for the adults and the kids will have sparkling juice.

For dessert, it's not traditional at all, but it's a decadent chocolate torte.

Typically, on Christmas day I prepare a late brunch with a spiral cut ham, a couple of different varieties of quiche, a cheesy potato breakfast casserole, kolache, (a Czech poppy-seed roll) fresh fruit, and fresh juices. Later in the day, we'll have some appetizers, leftover ham on finger rolls, warm up leftover potatoes, and we'll munch on whatever our hearts desire. There's always afternoon pie, but our Christmas day's are pretty relaxed around here!

As you can see, I do cover all 5 categories, but not necessarily in order! For many, our schedule would be a nightmare. For our family it just works. My point is that you can find out what works for you, too, just don't be afraid to shake things up a bit!

Back to the 5 categories, I'll cover each category individually and provide plenty of options, both simple and sinful!

Starters & Beverages

Let's face it, most of the time when I arrive at someone's house for a party I'm already starving! The best parties always have lots of finger foods readily available, along with great alcoholic and non-alcoholic beverage choices.

You can pull it all together easily, inexpensively, and provide some great options for your guest. Just follow a few simple guidelines to make sure that you have all of your bases covered.

 Want to throw an awesome party? Make sure that you have plenty of appetizers and plenty of beverages. Never let the food or drinks run out!

One of the most simple, make ahead appetizers that you can serve is a cheese platter. It's up to you how simple or gourmet you want to make it - most of the time it will depend on the tastes of your guests! I grew up on Colby and Monterey Jack served on a plate with Ritz crackers. As kids, we loved it! You can buy these favorite varieties of cheese already cut to cracker size in the refrigerator section of most grocery stores.

If your guest list is a bit more swanky, you'll want to work a little harder on your selections. If you're keeping things simple, I recommend that you have one soft cheese, like a Camembert or Brie; and one firm cheese, like a Manchego or Gruyere.

Serve the soft cheese with slices of baguette, or flavored crackers if your cheese is particularly mild. Apple slices, sun-dried tomatoes and some warm pistachios are prefect pairings for soft cheese.

Hard cheeses work very well with spicier foods, like horseradish, mustard or a spicy salami. Serve with a rye crisp or a seeded cracker.

All cheese varieties taste great with fresh fruits like strawberries, pears, and grapes, or dried fruits like apricots and figs. You might also include a small dish of olives and a few varieties of nuts to round out your cheese platter.

If you'd like to go a bit more exotic, there are lots of options available at your local cheese monger, or you can order cheese online from many sources and have it delivered to your door just a few days before your gathering.

How to Make a Cheese Platter

Try to include a variety of textures and flavors in your cheese platter. Most cheese belongs to one of six basic categories: aged, soft, semi-soft, firm, or blue. For a good variety, choose at least one from each group.

Some examples:
1. Fresh: Feta, Chevre, Cream Cheese
2. Aged: Aged Cheddar, Comte, Goat Gouda
3. Soft: Brie, Camembert, Brillat-Savarin
4. Semi-Soft: Colby, Havarti, Monterrey Jack
5. Firm: Manchego, Swiss, Gruyere, Parmesan
6. Blue: Gorgonzola, Roquefort, Stilton

How to Make a Cheese Platter

I would recommend that you serve at least one cheese that is familiar to many of your guests so that they aren't confused by the options, and if there will be young children, perhaps you could prepare them their own simple platter. Include awesome, kid-friendly favorites like fresh mozzarella, marbled Colby with Monterrey Jack, or an American Cheese spread.

For a party in which cheese is the main event, plan on buying 3 pounds for 8 people, 6 pounds for 16, or 9 pounds for 24. If cheese is one of many items being served, plan on buying 3 to 4 ounces per person.

Pairings

To accompany the cheese, I like to offer a selection of breads, including sliced baguette, bread sticks, and crackers in all different shapes and sizes.

It is recommended that you serve flavored crackers with mild cheeses as the cheese will accentuate the flavor in the cracker, serve seedy crackers with cheeses such as goat's cheese, slices of baguette work well with soft, easily spreadable cheeses such as brie. Apple slices pair well with Brie and Camembert, as do sun-dried tomatoes and warm pistachios.

 Making a cheese platter sounds like a lot of work, but much of it can be done in advance. It's a simple way to serve an elegant appetizer.

Edamame, maple syrup, and honey are interesting and delicious accompaniments to soft, fresh cheeses such as feta. Try serving praline bacon or nut brittle with your blue cheeses. Thinly-sliced onions are also an excellent complement to blues or pungent double/triple cream cheeses like Taleggio or St. Andre.

Serve hard cheeses with slightly spicy foods such as horseradish, mustard, or a spicy salami.

All cheese varieties taste fabulous with fresh fruit like strawberries, pears and grapes, or dried fruit like apricots and figs. You might also include a small dish of ripe olives and a few varieties of nuts.

Complete your platter with a meat choice or two, like prosciutto, smoked salmon, shrimp, or a spicy salami.

Serving Tips

Separate strong-smelling cheeses. If you want to serve a pungent, stinky-cheese, place it on a separate plate so it doesn't overpower more delicate ones. Four or five choices are enough variety.

Set out a separate knife for each cheese, especially the soft varieties. Soft cheese spreads well with a butter knife; firm cheese might require a paring knife; and aged cheese often requires a cheese plane.

Remove the cheese from the refrigerator an hour before serving—cold mutes flavor.

Spread out the spread. Place the cheese platters and the other nibbles on several tables to avoid guest gridlock. You could even put each cheese with it's suggested accompaniments on a separate platter!

Label each cheese so you won't need to recite the names all evening. If you like, also jot down a few poetic adjectives describing its flavor.

It sounds like making a cheese platter is a lot of work, but it's really not. The beautiful thing is that you can prepare much of it several days in advance and not give it a second thought!

That's a LOT of information about cheese! Here's the deal. If you can put together an awesome spread of cheese and fruit, you can entertain **anyone** with no worries. It's worth taking some time to do it right!

Date, Walnut & Blue Cheese Ball

4 oz crumbled Blue Cheese
1 Tbsp nonfat buttermilk
8 oz cream cheese, softened
3 Tbsp minced, pitted dates
1 Tbsp minced shallots
1/2 tsp grated lemon rind
1/4 tsp kosher salt
1/4 tsp black pepper
1/4 c minced fresh flat-leaf parsley
2-1/2 Tbsp chopped walnuts, toasted

Place blue cheese, buttermilk and cream cheese in a large bowl; beat with mixer at medium speed 2 minutes or until smooth and creamy.

Add dates, shallots, lemon rind, salt, and pepper; beat at medium speed until well blended, scraping sides of bowl as necessary.

Spoon cheese mixture onto a large sheet of plastic wrap. Form into a ball, suing a rubber spatula. Wrap cheese ball in plastic wrap; chill overnight.

Combine parsley and walnuts in a shallow dish. Unwrap cheese ball; gently roll in nut mixture, coating well. Place on serving plate. Serve immediately or cover and refrigerate until ready to serve.

More Starters

Ideally, you'll have a variety of appetizers when you're entertaining. Here are some of the different types of appetizers, but you certainly don't need to have one from each category. It's just to give you a few ideas.

1. Garden: Raw, cooked & stuffed veggies, potatoes, olives, fruits and berries.

   Try assembling your vegetables upright in glasses instead of on a tray. It's a unique way to present crudites that looks beautiful.

   Serve a variety of vegetables. Rather than serving just carrots and celery, add cucumber slices, sweet red and yellow peppers. If you can find them, add some fresh royal purple green beans for dipping!

2. Starch: Finger sandwiches, canapes, pizza, dumplings & filled phyllo pastry. Also bruschetta, breadsticks, crackers, biscotti, rolls and buns.

3. Protein: Meat & fish dishes like meatballs, sliced or skewered meats, chicken wings, eggs & cheese.

   Meatballs, shrimp, and any other type of meat is best served on a skewer for the convenience of your guests. Everyone can pick up their portion using the skewer instead of their fingers.

Chicken wings, bbq ribs and the like are very messy appetizers and best saved for another occasion like a backyard summer picnic.

4. Snacks: Nuts, chips, pretzels, tortilla chips, popcorn and other savory finger foods.

   These are the easiest appetizers of all. Small dishes of spiced or glazed nuts are delicious and pack a punch of protein. Pretzels and chips are a perfect carrier for any sort of dips that you have, and the saltiness are great with beer or tart cocktails like margaritas.

5. Dips & Spreads: To combine with other categories, try flavored butters, tepenades, pates, guacamole, relish and other spreads.

6. Sweets: Don't forget to have a few sweet things available, like chocolates or small cookies.

Festive Cracker Spread

1 (8 oz) pkg cream cheese, softened
1 (8 oz) pkg finely shredded
  sharp Cheddar cheese
1/2 c mayonnaise
3/4 c chopped pimento-stuffed olives
1/2 c chopped celery
1/3 c chopped onion
1/4 c chopped green bell pepper
2 tsp dried parsley

Beat the cream cheese, cheddar cheese, and mayonnaise with an electric mixer in a bowl until smooth.

Fold in the olives, celery, onion, bell pepper, and parsley; mixing just enough to evenly combine.

Cover and chill for at least 1 hour.

When it's cold outside, it's great if you can have at least one appetizer that is served warm.

Trader Joes has an awesome assortment of oven ready appetizers – from phyllo dough squares to warm dips and spreads – or you can make your own.

Sometimes you just don't have the space in your oven. Don't forget about your crock pot! Not only is it great for preparing an appetizer, but if your crock pot is cute (and there are some SUPER cute ones out there) you can serve it up right out of the pot, too! You don't have to worry about reheating it if it gets cool because it'll stay warm as long as you want. Does it get much easier than that?

Slow Cooker Artichoke & Spinach Dip

1 box (9 oz) frozen spinach,
  thawed, squeezed to drain
1 can (14 oz) quartered artichoke
  hearts, drained, chopped
1/2 c alfredo pasta sauce
1/2 c mayonnaise
3/4 tsp garlic salt
1/4 tsp pepper
1 c shredded Swiss cheese (4 oz)
1 loaf (20 inch length) baguette
  French bread, cut into 40 slices

Mix all ingredients except for the bread in a 1 to 1-1/2 quart slow cooker. Cover and cook on low heat setting for 2 to 4 hours. Serve with sliced bread.

Slow Cooker Greek Beef Bites

3 lbs. Beef boneless chuck roast,
trimmed of fat
2 Tbsp olive oil
4 cloves garlic, finely chopped
1 Tbsp dried oregano leaves
1 tsp salt
1/2 tsp ground black pepper
4 Tbsp grated lemon peel
1 c plain yogurt
1/2 small cucumber, peeled, cored
and finely chopped
1/2 tsp salt

Cut beef into 1 to 1-1/2" pieces. Heat oil
in a skillet over medium heat. Cook
beef in oil, in batches if necessary, 8 to
10 minutes, turning occasionally, until
brown on all sides.

Place beef in 3-4 quart slow cooker.
Sprinkle with garlic, oregano, salt,
pepper & lemon peel; toss to mix.
Cover and cook on low for 4 to 5 hours.

Stir together yogurt, cucumber, 1/2 tsp
salt and remaining lemon peel in small
bowl. Serve beef with toothpicks for
dipping into yogurt sauce. Beef bites
will hold on low heat for up to 2 hours.
Stir occasionally.

Beverages

Having a variety of beverage options, both alcoholic and non-alcoholic, available is so important to the success of any gathering. There are as many options as you can imagine, but to keep things simple I've listed just a handful of ideas.

Wine is always a great choice when it comes to choosing a beverage to accompany a holiday dinner. A Syrah is a medium bodied wine that is great with food or on its own. Hogue Cellars and Wyndham Estate are top Syrah producers to try.

My favorite wine is a Red Zinfandel and you can get a great bottle of Bogle Old Vine Zin for about $10. Ravenswood makes another good Red Zinfandel and their Vintner's Blend is only about $8 a bottle.

Sparkling fruit juice is delicious, and most have no refined sugar, caffeine or artificial flavors, which makes them a perfect choice when you're entertaining. IZZE is a great brand that has a variety of flavors available, like sparkling pomegranate, grapefruit and ginger. They are great on their own, and they make a great mixer for cocktails!

A Christmas punch is an inexpensive way to serve a crowd. It's easy to make one batch with alcohol and one batch without for the kids or adults who don't drink, and there are a lot of ways that you can make it special.

Blackberry Mojito Punch

3 c blackberry juice blend
2 (12 oz) cans frozen mojito mix
2 (1-liter) bottles club soda, chilled
3 limes, sliced
1 (12 oz) pkg frozen blackberries
fresh mint sprigs
1-1/2 c white rum (if desired)

Stir together juice blend, mojito mix, club soda, and sliced limes. Add rum for adults who would like to have an alcoholic beverage.

Serve with frozen blackberries and garnish with fresh mint sprigs.

Holiday Citrus Punch

2 c bottled pear nectar
4 c orange juice
2 c chilled club soda
Orange slices
1 c light rum (if desired)

Combine pear nectar and orange juice. Just before serving, stir in club soda and, if desired, light rum.

Pour into glasses over ice; garnish with orange slices.

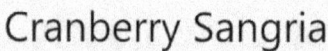

Cranberry Sangria

2 c fresh or frozen cranberries
1 c sugar
1 c water
1 (750 mL) bottle fruity red wine
1/2 c brandy
1 c fresh orange juice

fresh cranberries, orange, lemon
and lime slices to garnish

Bring cranberries, sugar and water to a boil in a medium sized saucepan over medium-high heat. Reduce heat to low, and simmer 5 minutes or until cranberries pop. Pour mixture through a wire-mesh strainer into a bowl, using the back of a spoon to squeeze out juice. Discard solids.

Transfer cranberry mixture to a large pitcher. Stir in wine, brandy, and orange juice. Chill 2 hours.

Serve over ice; garnish with cranberries and fruit slices, if desired.

To serve as a warm mulled cocktail, transfer mixture to a Dutch oven and heat just until it begins to boil. Garnish, if desired.

When it comes to starters, it's really just about making your guests comfortable when they arrive.

If your focus is going to be on your main dish, keep the appetizers simple, but plentiful. If you're serving appetizers only at your soiree, make sure that you have a nice variety of things to nosh on! Keep the appetizer dishes full, the cocktail glasses full, and everyone will surely have a wonderful time.

Sides

For a lot of people, the sides are the best part of the holiday meal. Mashed potatoes, green bean casserole, stuffing, cranberry sauce; it's easy to see why we love the side dishes.

Great side dishes not only complement your main course, but they also can be a great alternative for any vegetarian guests that will be joining you for the holidays.

There are plenty of options for quick and easy side dishes. The classics are always the best way to keep everyone happy, but I like to add a few surprises!

Here are recipes for a few classics that have a fresh twist. Since there was a Greek beef tips appetizer, I am also including a light orzo Greek salad recipe here that would be a nice addition to the heavier mashed potatoes and green bean casserole.

Green Bean Casserole

1-1/2 lbs green beans,
   trimmed and halved crosswise
2 Tbsp olive oil
3 c chopped sweet onion
1 tsp chopped fresh thyme
8 oz shitake mushrooms,
   stemmed & sliced
1 (8 oz) pkg button mushrooms
1/3 c Madeira wine or dry sherry
1/4 tsp salt
1/4 tsp freshly ground black pepper
3 Tbsp all-purpose flour
1 c chicken broth
1 c canned fried onions
1/2 c grated fresh Parmesan cheese

Preheat oven to 425°. Place beans in boiling water; cook 4 minutes. Drain, rinse, drain; set aside.

Heat a large skillet over medium-high heat. Add oil, onion & thyme; saute 4 minutes. Add mushrooms; saute 10 minutes or until liquid almost evaporates. Stir in wine, salt, & pepper; cook 2 minutes. Stir in flour; cook 1 minute, stirring constantly. Gradually stir in chicken broth; bring to a boil. Cook 1 minute or until thick, stir constantly.

Add mixture to green beans; toss well. Place in a 2-qt baking dish. Top with fried onions & cheese. Bake at 425° for 17 minutes or until top is lightly browned.

Ranch Mashed Potatoes

13 c cubed red potato
(about 4 pounds)
1/2 c reduced-fat sour cream
1/4 c chopped green onions
1/4 c low-fat buttermilk
3 Tbsp butter, softened
3/4 tsp salt
3/4 tsp dried basil
3/4 tsp dried oregano
1/2 tsp garlic powder
1/2 tsp freshly ground black pepper
1/4 tsp dried dill

Place potatoes in a Dutch oven; cover with water. Bring to a boil. Reduce heat, and simmer 20 minutes or until tender; drain. Place potato in a large bowl. Add sour cream and remaining ingredients; mash with a potato masher to desired consistency.

Greek Orzo Salad

1-1/2 c uncooked orzo pasta
2 (6 oz) cans artichoke hearts
1 tomato, seeded and chopped
1 cucumber, seeded and chopped
1 red onion, chopped
1 c crumbled feta cheese
1 (2 oz) can black olives, drained
1/4 c chopped fresh parsley
1 Tbsp lemon juice
1/2 tsp dried oregano
1/2 tsp lemon pepper

Bring a large pot of water to a boil.
Add pasta and cook for 8 to 10
minutes or until aldente; drain.

Drain artichoke hearts, reserving
liquid. In large bowl combine pasta,
artichoke hearts, tomato, cucumber,
onion, feta, olives, parsley, lemon
juice, oregano, and lemon pepper.

Toss and chill for 1 hour in
refrigerator. Just before serving,
drizzle reserved artichoke marinade
over salad.

*TIP You can prepare this the day
before... just reserve the feta and
tomato and add them with the
artichoke marinade just before
serving.

Keep It Simple Stuffing

3/4 c unsalted butter plus more for baking dish
1 lb, good quality, day old white bread, cubed
2-1/2 c chopped yellow onions
1-1/2 c 1/4" sliced celery
1/2 c chopped flat-leaf parsley
2 Tbsp chopped fresh sage
1 Tbsp chopped fresh rosemary
1 Tbsp chopped fresh thyme
2 tsp kosher salt
1 tsp freshly ground black pepper
2-1/2 c low-sodium chicken broth
2 large eggs

Preheat oven to 250°F. Butter a 13x9x2" baking dish; set aside. Scatter bread in a single layer on a rimmed baking sheet. Bake, stirring occasionally, until dried out, about 1 hour. Let cool; transfer to a very large bowl.

Melt 3/4 cup butter in a large skillet over medium-high heat; add onions & celery. Stirring just til brown, about 10 minutes. Add to bread; stir in herbs, salt, & pepper. Drizzle in 1 1/4 cups broth & toss. Let cool.

Preheat oven to 350°F. Whisk 1 1/4 cups broth & eggs in small bowl. Fold into bread gently until combined well. Transfer to baking dish, cover with foil, and bake 40 minutes.

Dressing can be made 1 day ahead.

Perfect Cranberry Sauce

1 (12 oz) bag fresh or frozen
  cranberries
1 c sugar
1 strip orange or lemon zest
2 Tbsp water

Empty bag of fresh or frozen cranberries into a saucepan and transfer 1/2 cup to a small bowl. Add sugar, orange or lemon zest and water to the pan and cook over low heat, stirring occasionally, until the sugar dissolves and the cranberries are soft, about 10 minutes.

Increase the heat to medium and cook until the cranberries burst, about 12 minutes. Reduce the heat to low and stir in the reserved cranberries. Add sugar, salt and pepper to taste and cool to room temperature before serving.

Main Dishes

Whether you choose to center your meal around a perfectly glazed ham, a tenderloin of beef, an apple cider brined turkey, or a grilled salmon is completely up to you. Anything goes! Depending on the type of dinner that you're planning, potluck, buffet, or a sit down dinner, you can make your entree choice work. More on that later...

If the traditional roast turkey is not your style, there are other non-traditional favorites that you could opt for. Consider a hearty lasagne for your Christmas eve dinner. How about a delicious Chinese buffet for Christmas day? Whatever your family's favorites might be, you can embrace them for your holiday meals.

Perhaps you're looking for something really special for your Christmas dinner. I've included recipes for a few main-course entrees that will make your holiday meal one to remember, including a delicious beef filet with mushroom sauce. Even though it's a perfect dish for entertaining, the leftovers are fabulous. (If you have any!)

There's also a stuffed pork tenderloin that is not only elegant, but juicy and full of flavor.

When your main dish is something really special, you can keep the sides simple and allow that main course to really be the star of your Christmas dinner.

Beef Filets with Mushroom Sauce

1/2 oz dried porcini mushrooms
2 c boiling water
1-1/2 tsp olive oil
1/3 c thinly sliced shallots
4 oz sliced fresh cremini
   mushroom caps (about 2 c)
2 garlic cloves, minced
salt & pepper
1/4 tsp black pepper
1/2 c pinot noir
2 Tbsp all-purpose flour
2 Tbsp chopped fresh sage
1 Tbsp chopped fresh thyme

Beef ingredients:
1 Tbsp olive oil
6 (4 oz) beef tenderloin steaks
salt and black pepper

Place porcini mushrooms in a bowl. Cover with 2 c. boiling water. Let sit 15 minutes. Drain through a sieve over a bowl, reserving mushrooms & liquid. Heat large pan over med-high heat. Add 1-1/2 tsp oil; swirl to coat. Add shallots; saute 1 minute. Add cremini mushrooms; saute 2 min or until almost tender. Add garlic; saute 30 seconds. Stir in porcini, salt & pepper; saute 1 min. Add wine to pan; bring to a boil. Cook until liquid almost evaporates (about 3 min). Sprinkle 2 Tbsp flour over mixture; cook 1 min. Gradually add the reserved mushroom liquid, stirring constantly. Simmer 2 min, stirring frequently. Stir in herbs.

Heat a large skillet over medium-high heat. Add 1 Tbsp oil. Sprinkle beef with salt & pepper. Add beef to pan; saute 4 minutes on each side. Remove from pan; let stand 10 minutes.

Spinach Stuffed Pork Tenderloin

2 (1 pound each) pork tenderloins
1 tsp celery salt, divided
1 tsp garlic powder, divided
1 tsp pepper, divided
8 slices provolone cheese
4 c. fresh spinach
4 thin slices deli ham

Cut a lengthwise slit down the center of each tenderloin to within 1/2" of bottom. Open tenderloin so it lies flat. On each half, make another, lengthwise slit down the center to within 1/2" of bottom; cover with plastic wrap. Flatten to 1/4" thickness. Remove plastic wrap; sprinkle pork with 1/4 tsp celery salt, 1/4 tsp garlic powder & 1/4 tsp pepper. Layer with the cheese, spinach & ham. Press down gently. Roll up jelly-roll style, starting with a long side. Tie the roast at 1-1/2" to 2" intervals with kitchen string. Sprinkle with remaining celery salt, garlic powder and pepper. Place on a rack in a shallow baking pan.

Bake, uncovered, at 425° for 25-30 minutes or until a meat thermometer reads 160°. Transfer to a serving platter. Let stand for 10 minutes before slicing.

Classic Easy Lasagna

1 lb ground beef
1 jar (24 oz) spaghetti sauce
1-1/2 c water
1 container (15 oz) ricotta
2 c shredded mozzarella
1/2 c grated parmesan
2 eggs
1/4 c chopped fresh parsley
1/2 tsp salt
1/4 tsp ground black pepper
9 pieces lasagna, uncooked

Pre-heat oven to 350°F. In 2-quart saucepan over medium-high heat, brown meat; drain. Add spaghetti sauce and water; simmer about 10 minutes. Meanwhile, in medium bowl, stir together ricotta cheese, one-half mozzarella cheese, Parmesan cheese, eggs, parsley, salt and pepper. Pour about 1 cup sauce on bottom of 11x7inch baking dish. Arrange 3 uncooked pasta pieces lengthwise over sauce; cover with 1 cup sauce. Spread one-half cheese filling over sauce. Repeat layers of pasta, sauce and cheese filling. Top with layer of pasta and remaining sauce; sprinkle with mozzarella cheese. Cover with foil. Bake 45 minutes. Remove foil; bake additional 10 minutes or until hot and bubbly. Let stand 10 minutes before cutting.

Rib Roast with Herb Crust

2 tablespoons sour cream
2 teaspoons prepared horseradish
Coarse salt and ground pepper
1 cup fresh breadcrumbs
1/4 cup extra-virgin olive oil
1/4 cup chopped fresh thyme,
    rosemary, and sage
1 garlic clove, chopped
2 teaspoons vegetable oil
1 boneless rib-eye roast
    (2 1/2 pounds), room temperature

Preheat oven to 400. In a small bowl, combine sour cream and horseradish; season with salt and pepper. In another bowl, combine breadcrumbs, olive oil, herbs, and garlic; season with salt and pepper.

In a large skillet, heat vegetable oil over medium-high. Season roast with salt and pepper; sear until browned on all sides, 10 minutes. Transfer to a cutting board. Spread sour cream mixture on one side of roast; top with breadcrumb mixture, pressing to adhere. Return roast to skillet or transfer to a rimmed baking sheet. Place in oven; cook until medium-rare or an instant-read thermometer inserted in center reads 140, 35 to 45 minutes. Let rest 15 minutes before slicing.

Desserts

A few special treats are wonderful to have when celebrating the holidays, but baking dozens of different types of cookies, candies, cakes and more is just too much. Who needs it? Not only is all of that sugar not good for you, but the amount of work that goes into all of that baking is way too much to add to your holiday plate (pun intended).

I love the basic cookie dough recipe that you make and from that dough you can make all kinds of different varieties of cookies. What an awesome idea if you want to have lots of variety without a lot of work. Here's my favorite basic cookie dough recipe from Good Housekeeping:

Basic Cookie Dough

2-3/4 c all-purpose flour
1/4 tsp baking soda
1/4 tsp salt
1 c (2 sticks) butter, softened
3/4 c granulated sugar
1 large egg
1 tsp vanilla extract

On waxed paper, combine flour, baking soda, and salt. In large bowl, with mixer on medium speed, beat butter and sugar 1 minute or until creamy, occasionally scraping bowl with rubber spatula. Add egg and vanilla; beat until well mixed. Reduce speed to low; gradually beat in flour mixture just until blended, occasionally scraping bowl.

Follow directions for your choice of cookie. Choose from:

- Fig-Filled Moons
- Chocolate Pinwheels
- Chewy Fruit Bars
- Butter Cookie Cutouts
- Hazelnut-Chocolate Sandwich Cookies
- Cranberry-Orange Spice Cookies
- Apple Pie Spice Rugelach
- Gingerbread Cutouts
- Mexican Wedding Cookies
- Chocolate-Dipped Peppermint Sticks
- Chocolate Raspberry Thumbprints
- Stained Glass Ornaments

Fig Filled Moons

Basic Cookie Dough
1 large orange
5 oz dried figs, stems removed
(about 1 cup)
1/2 c walnuts
1/4 c raisins
1/4 c honey
1-1/2 tsp ground cinnamon
1 large egg lightly beaten
Coarse sugar crystals (optional)

Prepare Basic Cookie Dough. Divide dough into 3 pieces. Flatten each into a disk; wrap each in plastic wrap. Refrigerate at least 2 hours, until firm enough to roll. Meanwhile, grate 1/2 tsp orange peel & squeeze 3 Tbsp. juice. In food processor with knife blade attached, combine orange peel and juice, figs, walnuts, raisins, honey, & cinnamon. Pulse until fig mixture is well blended but still has a coarse texture. Cover; set aside until ready to use.

Preheat oven to 350°F. Between 2 sheets of waxed paper, roll 1 disk of dough 1/8 inch thick. Remove top sheet. With floured 2 1/2-inch scalloped round biscuit cutter, cut out as many cookies as possible. Wrap and refrigerate trimmings to re-roll later. With spatula, carefully place cookies, 1" apart, on ungreased large cookie sheet. Spoon 1 level measuring tsp fig filling onto center of each cookie. Fold each cookie in half over filling; brush with egg. Sprinkle with sugar crystals.
Bake cookies 12-15 minutes or until tops are golden-brown. Transfer cookies to wire rack to cool. Repeat with remaining dough, dough trimmings, fig filling, & egg.

Chocolate Pinwheels

Basic Cookie Dough
1/3 c miniature semisweet chocolate chips
1/4 c confectioners' sugar
1 oz unsweetened chocolate, melted
2 Tbsp unsweetened cocoa powder
2 Tbsp all-purpose flour

Prepare Basic Cookie Dough. Divide in half; transfer half to another bowl. Stir chips, sugar, chocolate, and cocoa into half. Stir flour into plain dough. On sheet of waxed paper, roll chocolate dough into 14" by 10" rectangle. Repeat with plain dough. Turn over plain rectangle, still on waxed paper, and place, dough side down, on top of chocolate rectangle so that edges line up evenly. Peel off top sheet of waxed paper. Starting from long side, tightly roll rectangles together, jelly-roll fashion, to form log, lifting bottom sheet of waxed paper to help roll. Cut log crosswise in half. Wrap each half with plastic wrap and freeze 2 hours or refrigerate overnight.

Preheat oven to 350° F. With sharp knife, cut 1 log (keep other log refrigerated) crosswise into ¼ inch-thick slices. Place slices, 2 inches apart, on ungreased large cookie sheet. Bake cookies 10 to 12 minutes or until lightly browned. Transfer cookies to wire racks to cool. Repeat with remaining log.

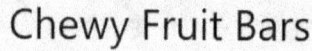

Chewy Fruit Bars

Basic Cookie Dough
3/4 tsp baking soda
1 tsp ground cinnamon
1-1/2 c packed dark brown sugar
2 large eggs
1 c walnuts, chopped
1 c pitted dried dates, chopped
1 c dried tart cherries
1/2 c dried apricot halves, chopped
1/2 c golden raisins
Confectioners' sugar for dusting
(optional)

Preheat oven to 350° F. Line a jelly-roll pan with foil, extending foil 2" above pan at ends; grease foil. Prepare Basic Cookie Dough, but in step 1, decrease flour to 2-1/2 cups, increase baking soda to 3/4 tsp total, and add cinnamon to flour mixture. In step 2, substitute 1-1/2 cups packed dark brown sugar for granulated sugar and use a total of 2 eggs. Add walnuts, dates, cherries, apricots, & raisins to dough, stirring until blended (dough will be thick).

With floured fingers, press dough evenly into prepared pan. Bake 25 to 28 minutes or until browned and toothpick inserted in center comes out clean. Cool completely in pan on wire rack. Remove from pan, using foil, and place on cutting board. With long, sharp knife, cut lengthwise into 4 strips, then cut each strip crosswise into 12 bars. Sprinkle with confectioners' sugar before serving, if you like.

Butter Cookie Cutouts

Basic Cookie Dough
Colored sugar crystals
Ornamental Frosting

Prepare Basic Cookie Dough: divide into 3 equal pieces. Flatten each piece into a disk, and wrap each in plastic wrap. Refrigerate at least 2 hours or overnight, until firm enough to roll.

Preheat oven to 350° F. Between 2 sheets of waxed paper, roll 1 disk of dough 1/8" thick. Remove top sheet of waxed paper. With floured 3" to 4" holiday-shaped cookie cutters, cut dough into as many cookies as possible; wrap and refrigerate trimmings. Place cookies, 1 inch apart, on ungreased large cookie sheet. Sprinkle with colored sugar if you like.

Bake cookies 11 to 13 minutes or until golden-brown. Transfer cookies to wire rack to cool. Repeat with remaining dough and trimmings. When cookies are cool, prepare Ornamental Frosting; use to decorate cookies. Set cookies aside to allow frosting to dry, about 1 hour.

Ornamental Frosting

1 pkg confectioners' sugar
3 Tbsp meringue powder
1/3 c warm water
Assorted food colorings (optional)

In bowl, with mixer on medium speed, beat sugar, meringue powder, and water until blended & mixture is very stiff, about 5 minutes. Tint frosting with food colorings. With small spatula or decorating bags with small writing tips, decorate cookies with frosting.

Hazelnut-Chocolate Sandwich Cookies

Basic Cookie Dough
1/3 c hazelnuts, toasted & chopped
3/4 c hazelnut-chocolate spread

Prepare Basic Cookie Dough. Preheat oven to 350° F. With hands, shape dough by level measuring ½ tsp into balls. Place balls, 2" apart, on ungreased large cookie sheet. Dip bottom of flat-bottomed glass in sugar as needed; use to press each ball into 1" round. Sprinkle half of the rounds with hazelnuts. Bake cookies 9 to 10 minutes or until edges are golden-brown. Transfer to wire rack to cool. Repeat. Assemble sandwich cookies: Spread flat sides of plain cookies with 1/2 teaspoon hazelnut-chocolate spread. Top each with a nut-covered cookie, top side up, pressing lightly.

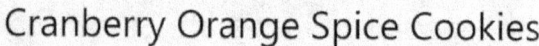

Cranberry Orange Spice Cookies

Basic Cookie Dough
1/2 c dried cranberries, finely chopped
1/4 c crystallized ginger, finely chopped
2 tsp grated fresh orange peel
1 tsp pumpkin pie spice
3 Tbsp green sugar crystals
3 Tbsp red sugar crystals

Prepare Basic Cookie Dough. In step 2, stir in cranberries, ginger, orange peel, & pumpkin pie spice along with flour until well mixed. Divide dough in half. On lightly floured surface, shape each half into 10" long log. Using hands or two clean rulers on sides, press each log into 10" long squared-off log. Wrap each in plastic wrap and freeze until firm enough to slice, 2 hours or refrigerate overnight. (Logs can be frozen up to 1 month.) Preheat oven to 350° F. On 1 sheet of waxed paper, place green sugar. Unwrap 1 log and press sides in sugar to coat. Cut log into 1/4" slices. Place slices, 1" apart, on ungreased large cookie sheet. Bake cookies 14 to 16 minutes or until golden. Transfer cookies to wire rack to cool. Repeat with red sugar and second log.

Apple Pie Spice Rugelach

Basic Cookie Dough
1/3 c all-purpose flour
1 c dried currants
2/3 c walnuts or pecans,finely chopped
1/4 c (packed brown sugar
1-1/2 tsp apple pie spice
3 Tbsp granulated sugar
1/2 c plus 1 Tbsp apple butter

Prepare Basic Cookie Dough, adding 1/3 c flour into dry ingredients in step 1. Divide dough into 4 equal pieces. Flatten each piece into a disk; wrap each with plastic wrap. Refrigerate dough 4 hours or overnight, until firm enough to roll. Meanwhile, in small bowl, mix currants, walnuts, brown sugar, and 1 tsp apple pie spice. In cup, mix granulated sugar with remaining 1/2 teaspoon apple pie spice. Preheat oven to 350° F. Between 2 sheets of waxed paper, roll 1 disk of dough into 9" round. Remove top sheet of waxed paper.

Spread dough round with 1 heaping measuring tablespoon apple butter; sprinkle with 1/2 c fruit mixture, leaving 1/4" border around edge. With pizza wheel or sharp knife, cut round into 12 wedges. (If dough becomes too soft to work with, place in refrigerator 10 to 15 minutes to firm up.)
Starting at curved edge, roll up each wedge jelly-roll fashion. Place cookies, point side down, 1 inch apart, on ungreased large cookie sheet; shape into crescents. Brush tops lightly with water and sprinkle with some spiced sugar.
Bake cookies 15 minutes or until golden-brown. Transfer cookies to wire rack to cool. Repeat with remaining dough, fruit mixture, and spiced sugar.

Gingerbread Cutouts

Basic Cookie Dough
1/2 tsp baking soda
2 tsp ground cinnamon
2 tsp ground ginger
1/2 tsp ground nutmeg
1/4 tsp ground cloves
3/4 c packed dark brown sugar
1/4 c dark (robust) molasses
Ornamental Frosting (optional)
Small red candies (optional)

Prepare Basic Cookie Dough, but in step 1, increase baking soda to 1/2 tsp total and add spices to flour mixture. In step 2, reduce butter to 1 stick, substitute dark brown sugar for granulated, and add molasses with egg and vanilla.

Divide dough into 3 equal pieces. Flatten each into a disk; wrap each in plastic wrap. Refrigerate dough 2 hours or overnight, until firm enough to roll.

Preheat oven to 350° F. Between 2 sheets of waxed paper, roll 1 disk of dough 1/8" thick. Remove top sheet of waxed paper. With floured 3- to 4-inch holiday-shaped cookie cutters, cut out as many cookies as possible; wrap and refrigerate trimmings. Place cookies, 1 inch apart, on ungreased large cookie sheet. Bake cookies 11 to 13 minutes or until edges begin to brown. Transfer cookies to wire rack to cool. Repeat with remaining dough and trimmings. When cookies are cool, prepare Ornamental Frosting if you like; add small red candies to decorate. Set cookies aside to allow frosting to dry, about 1 hour.

Mexican Wedding Cookies

1-1/2 c pecans
3 Tbsp confectioners' sugar, sifted
1-1/2 c confectioners' sugar, sifted
Basic Cookie Dough

In food processor with knife blade attached, pulse pecans with 3 Tbsp confectioners' sugar until very finely ground. Prepare Basic Cookie Dough, stirring ground pecans into flour mixture before adding to butter mixture. Preheat oven to 350° F. Shape dough by rounded tsp into 1" balls. Place balls, 1-1/2" apart, on ungreased cookie sheet.

Bake 13-15 minutes or until bottoms are browned & cookies are light golden. Let stand 2 min. to firm up slightly, then transfer to wire rack to cool. Repeat with remaining dough. Roll cooled cookies in confectioners sugar to coat; twice if desired.

Chocolate Dipped Peppermint Sticks

Basic Cookie Dough
1/4 tsp peppermint extract
Green and red paste food coloring
5 oz white chocolate, melted
6 green or red starlight mints, crushed

Prepare Basic Cookie Dough. Divide dough in half; transfer half to another bowl. Stir peppermint extract into 1 portion of dough. Divide peppermint dough in half; transfer half to another bowl. Tint 1 portion green, the other red. Preheat oven to 350° F. Line 9" by 9" metal baking pan with plastic wrap, extending wrap over 2 sides of pan. Pat plain dough in pan. Freeze 10 minutes. Pat green dough over half of plain dough; pat red dough over remaining plain dough. Freeze 10 min.

Lift dough from pan using plastic wrap. Cut dough into thirds so that one-third is all red on top, one-third is all green on top, and middle third is half red and half green. Cut each third crosswise into 3/8-inch strips. Twist strips and place, 1-1/2" apart, on ungreased cookie sheet. Bake 11 to 13 minutes or until golden-brown. Transfer to wire rack. Repeat. Dip one end of each cookie into chocolate and sprinkle chocolate with crushed mints. Refrigerate cookies 15 minutes to set.

Chocolate Raspberry Thumbprints

Basic Cookie Dough
2 oz unsweetened chocolate, melted
1/4 c unsweetened cocoa
1-1/4 c sliced almonds, coarsely chopped
1/2 c seedless red raspberry jam

Preheat oven to 350° F. Prepare Basic Cookie Dough. In step 2, beat in chocolate & cocoa with egg & vanilla extract. Shape dough by rounded tsp into 1" balls.

Place almonds on waxed paper; roll balls in chopped almonds. Place balls, 1-1/2" apart, on ungreased cookie sheet. With thumb, make small indentation in center of each ball. Fill each indentation with 1/4 tsp jam.

Bake cookies 14-15 minutes or until jam is bubbly & cookies are baked through. Transfer cookies to wire rack to cool. Repeat with remaining balls and jam.

Stained Glass Ornamental

Basic Cookie Dough
1 bag (6.25 oz) hard candy,
  such as sour balls

Prepare Basic Cookie Dough; divide into 3 pieces. Flatten each piece into a disk; wrap each in plastic wrap. Refrigerate at least 2 hours, until firm enough to roll. While dough is chilling, place hard candy in heavy-duty plastic bag. Place on towel-covered work surface. With mallet or rolling pin, lightly crush candy into small pieces about the size of coarsely chopped nuts, being careful not to crush until powdery.

Preheat oven to 350° F. Line large cookie sheet with foil. Between 2 sheets of waxed paper, roll 1 disk of dough 1/8" thick. Remove top sheet of waxed paper. With 3" - 4" holiday-shaped cookie cutters, cut out as many cookies as possible. Place 1" apart on prepared cookie sheet. Cut out centers of cookies with 1-1/2 – 2 inch cookie cutters. Remove and refrigerate trimmings and cutout centers. Bake cookies 7 minutes. Remove cookie sheet from oven; fill each cookie's center with 1/2 teaspoon crushed candy. Return to oven and bake 3 to 4 minutes longer or until cookies are lightly browned and candy is melted. Cool cookies on cookie sheet on wire rack. With metal spatula, remove cookies. Repeat with remaining dough, trimmings, and candy.

Cookie Swap Parties

Another option if you want to have a wide variety of treats to offer your guests, is to host a cookie swap party. It's a fun way to not only spend some time with friends over the holidays, but to make holiday baking easier for all of you!

You might think "the more the merrier" but you'll be better off if you keep it small. You'll want to have less than 20 friends, for sure, to make sure that everyone has a good time.

At the end of the day, you each end up with 7 or 8 dozen cookies. Never been to or hosted a cookie swap party? You can find lots of information online, and lots of inspiration on Pinterest!

How to Throw A Cookie Swap Party

Determine the guest list: Choose 10-20 friends who you think would be interested in sharing their baked goods with you. Ask them to bring 6 dozen of their favorite holiday cookies and to send you the recipe ahead of time.

Set the Date and Time: Pick a date and time that works best for you and for your guests' work and travel schedules. You'll want to have it close enough to the holidays so that the cookies are fresh, but not so late that you get caught up in the last-minute holiday rush. Usually about 10 days in advance works well.

Set some ground rules: Make sure that the instructions on the invitations are clear. Let your guests know how many cookies they should bring, when thy need to RSVP, and when to send in their recipes. Warn them to be flexible! You might have to ask them to make something different if you have 6 guests bringing the same type of cookies.

SAMPLE RULES:
Cookies should be homemade.
Cookies should be holiday themed.
Cookies should be shelf stable. (not requiring refrigeration)
No burnt cookies!

To prepare for the party, set your table with enough platters and pans to hold each guests cookies. Make it pretty! Mix in a few cake stands and some fresh flowers. You'll need enough tongs for each platter so that guests can make their selections without touching the cookies with their hands.

Use place cards to show what type of cookies are on each platter and who brought them.

Provide inexpensive paper bakery boxes and festive twine for guests to package and take home their cookies - several smaller boxes are better than one large box!

Provide snacks and refreshments. The best part of a cookie swap party is always the WINE! Serve appetizers and finger foods so that guests can sip, nosh, and have fun!

Extras

Bread and rolls are my biggest downfall during the holidays. I can't resist eating too many rolls, especially when it comes to the Czech pastries that I make every year called kolache.

Kolache are one of the few things that I make every single holiday. It's just not Christmas without them! I cheat a little when I make kolache, but I learned the shortcut from my mom, so I know it's okay. Her cheat? Buy frozen loaves of bread dough, let them defrost and cut each loaf into12 pieces. Flatten each piece into a 3-4" square and put a teaspoon of poppyseed filling in the center of each square of dough. Fold two opposite corners and pinch to seal, then the other two corners. Bake at 350° for 40 minutes. You can use any other sort of filling if you don't care for poppyseed. Almond filling is amazing, as is lemon, apple and prune. With a dab of butter while they are still warm, kolache are absolutely amazing.

 Skip the rolls? Heck no! If you have guest that are avoiding gluten, offer an alternative, but you should always offer bread for others!

I also love what my bakery calls "finger rolls." They are a rectangular shape that is perfect for making small sandwiches. They are white, super soft, and delicious.

You might opt for a crusty baguette, a soft, hearty rye roll, muffins, challah, or whatever else compliments your main-course. If you're serving the beef filets with mushroom sauce, the perfect accompaniment is a parmesan popover. They are easy and impressive!

Parmesan Popovers

1 c fat-free milk
2 large eggs
4.5 oz all-purpose flour (about 1 c)
1/2 tsp kosher salt
cooking spray
2 Tbsp grated Parmesan Cheese

Heat oven to 400°. Combine milk & eggs in a bowl. Weigh or lightly spoon flour into a dry measuring cup; level with a knife. Add flour and salt to milk mixture, stirring well; let stand 30 minutes. Place popover tin in oven for 5 minutes. Remove tin from oven; lightly coat popover cups with cooking spray. Spoon 1/4 cup batter into each cup, and sprinkle with cheese. Bake at 400° for 35 minutes or until puffed and golden. Makes 6 popovers.

30 Minute Rolls

1 c plus 2 Tbsp warm water
1/3 c oil
2 Tbsp active dry yeast
1/4 c sugar
1 1/2 tsp salt
1 egg
3 1/2 c bread flour

Heat oven to 400°. In your mixer bowl combine the water, oil, yeast and sugar and allow it to rest for 15 minutes. Using your dough hook, mix in the salt, egg and flour. Knead with hook until will incorporated and dough is soft and smooth. (Just a few minutes)

Form dough into 12 balls and then place in a greased 9 x 13 pan and allow to rest for 10 minutes. Bake for 10 minutes at 400 degrees or until golden brown.

Potluck, Buffet, or Sit-Down Celebration?

Whether you choose to have a potluck dinner and have everyone bring a dish to share, serve your dinner buffet style, or have a sit-down dinner is completely up to you. Depending on what you decide, you might alter your menu choices.

Potluck

For a potluck, you'll want to manage the food that will be served by assigning categories or even specific dishes to certain people. You may decide to provide the main course yourself and ask guests to fill in with appetizers, side dishes, desserts, and extras.

As the host of a potluck dinner, you should always provide:

- utensils, napkins, plates, and cups
- ice and beverages
- seasonings and condiments

 When you're hosting a potluck, have a few easy backup dishes on hand in case the food runs low. Better safe than sorry!

If you don't mind a certain amount of risk, let your guests be creative in the dishes that they bring. You'll end up with a fun variety of dishes that you may not have had if you requested specific foods.

You may want to have a few easy backup dishes on hand in case the food runs low. Things like frozen appetizers, fresh veggies, lettuce salad, and instant potatoes can be added to the mix quickly if a guest has to cancel at the last minute.

Another tip is to touch base with guests that are bringing bigger things to the potluck the day before the event. You don't need to come right out and ASK, but you could! A quick "Just checking in to see how the food prep is going. Are you managing okay?" should suffice!

Buffet

A buffet works well for both casual and more formal meals. The food is arranged on a table or a sideboard and guests serve themselves.

If you have enough space, pull the table or sideboard out from the wall so that guests can serve themselves from both sides.

A pretty tablecloth or runner will create a festive looking buffet, along with a few small decorative items like mildly scented fresh flowers, candles, or a low centerpiece.

Once you have determined how the traffic will flow, set plates at the beginning of the buffet and napkins and utensils at the end. That way, your guests won't have to worry about carrying utensils while trying to fill their plates. To make things even easier, roll the utensils in the napkins.

Arrange the food in the order in which it will be eaten: appetizers, main course, side dishes and so on. Put cold dishes before hot ones & be sure to have serving utensils for each dish.

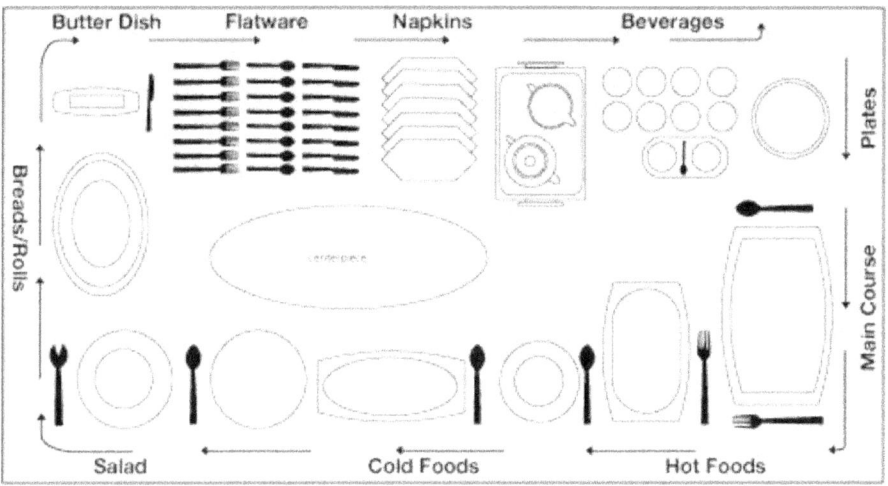

For a beautiful buffet, place food at different levels. It makes the table seem less crowded and guests are able to easily see every dish.

You can used tiered serving platters or stack cake stands to fit more food in a smaller area. Use pedestals or footed bowls, or you can put boxes under the tablecloth to give a platter some height.

A great way to keep traffic flowing is to set up a separate table for desserts and beverages and place it away from the main buffet.

Sit Down Dinner

A sit down dinner works well for a casual, family style meal or a more formal dinner. The perfect number for a sit down dinner is six to eight people. You want festive conversation, but not so many people that the conversations are always split up.

Serving the appetizers in the living room or family room give you a little extra time to set the table or finish preparing the main course. It also gives guests the freedom to begin eating before all of the guests have arrived.

Use unscented candles, groupings of low cut, mildly scented, fresh flowers and a tablecloth or runner to make a beautiful table without a lot of effort. Candlelight creates ambiance that you just can't get from overhead lighting.

Set everything up nicely, but don't be stuffy. Make sure that your tablecloth can handle a few spills so that you don't have to worry about it throughout the meal. Guests will be able to relax and will enjoy themselves more in a beautiful but casual setting.

Finally, don't be in a hurry to clear the table when everyone has finished eating. If you clear too soon, it can break up conversations and can be a cue for guests to leave. Lingering encourages relaxing. Just keep the wine flowing!

Breakfast

Lunch

Dinner

European

Formal

Banquet or Brunch

Special Diet Solutions

Lactose intolerant, gluten sensitive, vegetarian, paleo... how do you cook to accommodate a guest with special dietary needs?

Bringing an appetizer or dessert to share when you visit someone's home over the holidays is a very nice gesture, but it can be tricky. With friends and family that are vegetarian, gluten sensitive, sugar free, or dieting, it can be incredibly challenging to bring a dish that everyone is able to eat, and that everyone will enjoy!

Here are some easy appetizers and desserts that you can put together in a hurry AND will satisfy a crowd:

Hummus is a delicious Mediterranean dip made from chickpeas, tahini, olive oil, lemon juice, salt and garlic. It's completely safe for vegetarian and gluten free diets. There is no sugar in it and it's fairly low calorie. I love to dip pita bread chips and veggies in hummus. Wellaby's makes gluten free pita chips that you could pair with the hummus to make it awesome for any gluten avoiders.

Corn chips and tortilla chips are also gluten free, so many of the chips from the grocery store aisle are safe for gluten avoiders. Chips with guacamole and salsa are always popular, and when it comes to bringing a dish to share, you really can't get much easier.

Of course there are a million recipes online for gluten free, sugar free, dairy free dishes and I would encourage you to look through and see if you can find something special that you'd like to prepare for your family this year. I can guarantee that those who have special dietary needs will appreciate your efforts.

Desserts are a bit more difficult than a side dish or appetizer. There is always fresh fruit, but if you're looking to make something a little bit more special, this flour-less chocolate cake is absolutely amazing.

Passover Flourless Cake

1 c (6 oz) chopped semisweet
   chocolate chips
1/2 c (1 stick, 4 oz) unsalted butter
3/4 c (5 1/4 oz) granulated sugar
1/8 tsp salt
1 - 2 tsp espresso powder, optional
3 large eggs
1/2 c unsweetened cocoa powder

Ingredients for Glaze:
1 c chopped semisweet chocolate
   chips
1/2 c heavy cream
1/4 c sliced almonds, toasted

Preheat oven to 375°F. Lightly grease 8" round cake pan; cut a piece of waxed paper to fit, grease & lay in the bottom of pan. Put chocolate & butter in microwave safe bowl & heat till butter is melted & chips are soft. Stir until chips melt. Transfer the melted chocolate/butter to mixing bowl. Add sugar, salt, & espresso powder. Add eggs, beating briefly until smooth. Add cocoa powder & mix to combine. Spoon the batter into the prepared pan. Bake the cake for 25 minutes; the top will have formed a thin crust. Remove it from the oven, and cool it in the pan for 5 minutes.

Loosen pan edges with knife & turn out on serving plate. Allow the cake to cool completely before glazing. To prepare the glaze: Combine the chocolate and cream in a microwave-safe bowl; Heat till the cream is very hot, but not simmering. Remove from microwave & stir till chocolate melts & the mixture is completely smooth. Spoon the glaze over the cake, spreading it to drip over the sides a bit. Allow the glaze to set for several hours before serving the cake.

If you don't know if any party attendees have special dietary needs, it's always best to serve a few things that are safe for almost everyone.

Nuts: Gluten Free, Dairy Free, Paleo Approved

Fruit: Berries, Apples, Pears, Citrus: Gluten Free, Dairy Free, Paleo Approved

Vegetables: Broccoli, Carrots, Cauliflower, Celery, Cucumber, Squash, Sweet Potatoes: Gluten Free, Dairy Free, Paleo Approved.

*TIP

Swap almond milk for regular milk in any recipe – you can't taste the difference but any guests that are lactose intolerant will appreciate it!

Pinterest is a great resource for recipes. I have hundreds posted on my boards at www.pinterest.com/LittleXMas.

The Hostess With the Mostess

Being the one to host your extended family gathering year after year is something that many dread. It's not just the expense of it - it's a lot of work! Planning, cooking and cleaning for days can leave you feeling overworked and under-appreciated when it's all said and done. But what can you do when you, for whatever reason, are the only one who can be the host during the holidays?

One of the biggest complaints that I heard while I was researching this book was that the host spends all day in the kitchen cooking and cleaning up while everyone else enjoys themselves.

Instead of refusing to host altogether, try to figure out how the cooking and cleanup afterward could be simplified enough to make hosting be okay. Once you've decided, then stick to your guns and do what it takes to make it work.

Here are some shortcuts that you might consider taking to help make your day more enjoyable:

- Use disposable plates, serving dishes, etc. when you can. We have a pretty "green" lifestyle, but when it comes to hosting a crowd I wouldn't think twice about choosing some nice disposable plates, roasting pans, baking sheets, glassware; anything that I could.

- Choose a simple menu. Instead of slaving over the stove, purchase a prepared meat & cheese tray with crackers, and a precooked, spiral sliced ham that just needs reheating. Serve it with a potato casserole that you can make ahead, bakery purchased rolls and pie. If anyone comments negatively, they are immediately volunteered for providing whatever it was that they complained about for next years party!

- Think outside the box. A large pan of lasagne can be made days in advance and reheated. Serve it with bagged salad - Pour a few bags of romaine in a large bowl, toss in some ripe olives, baby tomatoes, croutons and a sprinkle of parmesan cheese. Purchase breadsticks from your local bakery, brush them with melted butter and sprinkle them with garlic and fresh parmesan before reheating. For dessert, serve store bought pie, cake, or cookies.

- If your family is open to it, make your holiday dinner a potluck and ask everyone to bring a dish to share. You could have some fun with it by making it a contest! A chili cook-off is just one option. How about prizes like, "Best Appetizer Using 3 Ingredients or Less," "Best Dessert Besides Pie Made Using Store Bought Pie Crust," or "Best Beef Made Using Chuck Roast."

Being a Great Guest

When you're hosting a large gathering, it's a ton of work but at least you know what is expected of you. As a guest, sometimes people really don't know what to do.

If you want to be a great guest this Christmas, connect with the host a few weeks before your celebration and find out what you might bring. If they say that there isn't anything, dig a bit deeper. Find out what is being served and suggest that you could bring something to complement the main course. Offer to bring a cheese tray, appetizer, or fresh vegetables for everyone to munch on. Let them know that you have a fabulous bakery in your neighborhood and you'd be happy to pick up rolls or pie (or both).

If you are bringing a dish for a potluck, don't assume that you can arrive at the party and prep your dish at the already-busy kitchen. Bring it ready to go; and don't forget to bring serving utensils.

Gift ideas for the hostess? Wine and flowers are always nice. Chocolates are great, too. Or how about a gift card for a massage. Nice!

It's a nice gesture to bring a few bottles of wine, some chocolates, or even a festive bouquet of flowers for the host as a small gesture of your appreciation for the work that they have done.

Offer to help with the last minute tasks. Sometimes a host may be a bit of a control freak (like I can be when hosting). In that case, having another person in the kitchen can be more stressful than helpful.

One of the best things that a guest can do is to simply make themselves available. There are always things that the host needs help with – whether it's finding a few more chairs, stirring something on the stove, or help setting up the buffet. When that time comes, your help will certainly be appreciated.

When everyone has finished eating, suggest that the host sit and relax a while and visit while you clear the table.

Any effort that you make will certainly be appreciated by your host, and hopefully they will be able to spend more than a few minutes enjoying their day.

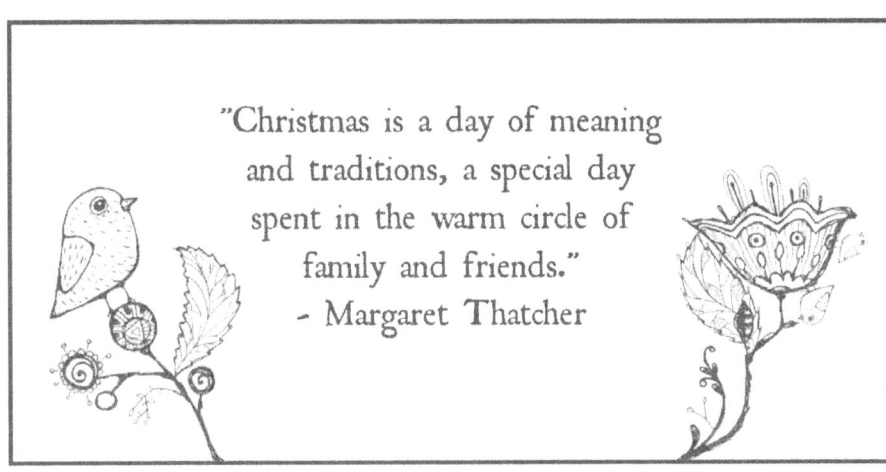

"Christmas is a day of meaning
and traditions, a special day
spent in the warm circle of
family and friends."
- Margaret Thatcher

Chapter 5
Family Matters

One of the biggest sources of holiday stress for many is family. The family dinner, dealing with extended family, the obligations, and the complications can turn your holidays into a nightmare.

The idea that holiday gatherings are supposed to be joyful, stress-free occasions is total fiction. Family relationships are complicated and sometimes the best you can do is prepare yourself for the worst, especially in cases where parents are divorced and remarried. A young family may feel obligated to visit 4 sets of parents each Christmas!

What's the best way to deal with family at Christmastime? You can opt out... or jump in with both feet! You get to pick.

Going Neither Here Nor There

One option, although it may sound extreme, is to opt out of the holiday family gatherings altogether. When my kids were little, this is exactly what I did and it was the best thing that I could have done. Instead of loading my very young children in the car on Christmas morning for a 90 minute drive to grandpa & grandma's house, we enjoyed a leisurely brunch and let them play with their toys from Santa.

I got plenty of flack from family at first, but we started a new tradition by spending time with my parents the weekend before Christmas. I will always treasure those memories! Instead of spending Christmas day with them and 40 to 50 other family members, we had them to ourselves and could actually enjoy visiting with each other, sharing a meal and exchanging gifts.

 Family traditions naturally evolve over the years. Don't be afraid to make the changes that you want to create a beautiful Christmas!

After a few years, other family members started doing the same thing. They wanted time with their immediate family, too! Eventually, mom and dad would visit one of their children on Christmas day instead of everyone going to their house.

Family traditions evolve over the years as families grow, children marry and have children of their own, and family members move out of the area. Don't be afraid to take a stand and let your needs and wishes known!

One Big Happy Family?

I was lucky to have a large family that was close – and where everyone got along! Not everyone can say the same.

Family gatherings can bring out the best in people, or the worst. Going home for the holidays can bring back some wonderful memories, but what if your childhood memories aren't all that wonderful?

When going home to a dysfunctional family, Martha Beck, along with several other social scientists, suggests that a good way to deal with a difficult family gathering over the holidays is to try to become an "observer" instead of getting wrapped up in family drama. There are different activities that you can do to protect yourself emotionally over the holidays by "observing" your family.

Queen for a Day

This little game is based on the old TV show in which four women competed to see who had the most miserable life. The contestant judged most pathetic got, among other things, a washing machine in which to cleanse her tear-stained clothing.

Martha Beck's version goes like this: Prior to a family function, arrange to meet with at least two friends—more, if possible—after the holidays. You'll each tell the stories of your respective family get-together, then vote to see whose experience was most horrendous. That person will then be crowned queen, and the others will buy her lunch.

Comedy Club

In this exercise, you look to your family not for love and understanding but for comedy material. The more atrocious your family's behavior is, the funnier it is in the re-telling. Watch pro comics to see the enormous fun they can have describing appalling marriages, ghastly parenting, or poisonous family secrets.

When you're back among friends, telling your own wild stories, you may find that you no longer suffer from your family's brand of insanity; you've actually started to enjoy it.

Dysfunctional Family Bingo

This one is my favorite of the games recommended by Martha Beck, though it involves considerable preparation. A few weeks before the holidays, gather with friends and provide each person with a blank bingo card. Each player fills in her bingo squares with dysfunctional phrases or actions that are likely to surface at her particular family party. For example, if you dread the inevitable "So when are you going to get married?" that question goes in one square of your bingo card. If your brother typically shows up crocked to the gills, put "Al is drunk" in another square, and so on.

Take your finished cards to your respective family gatherings. (DISCREETLY PLEASE!) Whenever you observe something that appears on your bingo card, mark off that square. The first person to get bingo should send a text to the group and announce their victory. If no one has a full bingo, the person who has the largest number of filled-out squares wins the game. The winner shall be determined at the post holiday meeting, where they will be granted the ever gratifying free lunch.

Dealing with Family Conflict

Holiday gatherings can put you in the same room as family members that you avoid the rest of the year, and that can set the stage for conflict. Promise yourself that you will not engage in any family drama. Remember that when someone points their finger at you, it's seldom actually about you, but instead about what they have in their own mind. Taking things personally only makes you easy prey. **Keep reminding yourself that it's not really about you. Take a deep breath.**

There are a few things that you can try to help you deal with any family member that you have difficulty communicating with:

- Ask a lot of questions. Keep them talking about themselves. Sometimes people just don't have good boundaries. If, for example, you bring a boyfriend home to meet the family for the first time and your aunt asks, "So, when are you two going to get married?" You could get embarrassed and explain that you just started dating, or you can turn it around and quickly respond with "How long did you and uncle date before you got married?"

- Use a little humor to diffuse the situation. Responding to her by saying something like "We actually got married yesterday and didn't want to say anything." Then just walk away.

- Without being too snarky, you can dismiss the question by laughing and saying something like "That's a highly personal question!" or "Am I under oath?" Sometimes a short answer will make them realize that they have crossed a line and they'll leave you alone.

Family is important, but whether you have a small family or a large extended family, there is no guarantee that everyone will get along! There's bound to be some family members you just connect with better than others. Sometimes just realizing that just because you're family doesn't mean you'll get along in every situation, share the same views, or even enjoy each others company!

When it comes to spending time during the holidays with family, pledge to be kind to everyone, be respectful of differing points of view, but be confident and assertive enough to move away from awkward conversations. Move toward family that you feel more comfortable spending time with. Set secure boundaries and be sure that you take good care of yourself and your needs.

Enjoying Family Time

How can you enjoy spending time with your family this year?

The key is to take control.

Could you bring along some board games and start an annual Yahtzee tournament?

Is there a person in particular that you're interested in conversing with? Send them an email or text before the holiday gathering and let them know that you're looking forward to seeing them!

Remember that you are not at the mercy of your relatives. If you continually do things that make yourself miserable over the holidays, ask yourself why. Make a list! Writing down the reasons why you keep up holiday traditions, and why you should or should not continue them can help clarify your situation and will remind you that you DO have a choice!

What would happen if you changed things up this year? Would your family be upset? Is that something that you could live with? What are the consequences for the short and long term?

What I'm trying to say here is that this year, make sure that you don't do things the same way as always just because that's the way that you always do them. If you're not happy with your old holiday traditions, then it's time to make some new ones!

Creating New Family Traditions

You don't need to spend hours trying to invent new things to do. Try picking the three most important family traditions and let the rest go this year. Your holiday schedule definitely doesn't need to be jam-packed with activities, and by keeping your calendar open, you'll free up time to be able to go out and try new things.

Adding a new holiday tradition isn't necessarily something that you consciously choose one year. It usually happens by accident when you do something one year, and then it happens again the next, and the next... There is no need to stress out over what new family tradition you'd like to add to your holidays.

For years, our holiday tradition was to watch the entire Star Wars Trilogy back to back on Christmas Day. Why? Because TNT aired all 3 movies every year, and there was really nothing else to do!

If there is a specific activity that you'd like to try this year, give it a shot and see how it goes. If it's something that everyone enjoys, odds are good that they will want to participate again next year and it will become a tradition. If not, then it will fall away and something new will replace it.

After the Loss of a Family Member

After the death of a family member, traditions can change dramatically. A gathering can be even more uncomfortable than usual if nobody knows what to do. Should you talk about the person who passed away? Should you avoid talking about him or her so that you don't upset anyone? Should you just watch football?

It can be good for everyone to get together and remember the deceased person. Families that can laugh and share stories can help each other heal. But rather than trying to continue old traditions without the person, try to make some new memories. Maybe this is the year that everyone spends the holidays at a resort, or meets at a restaurant for dinner.

Everyone feels the loss, but families often dance around the subject and it makes for a long, awkward day. That doesn't mean that you need to have a second memorial service or spend the day focused on loss, but saying "Mom's pie was always the best. I sure miss her this time of year." is not only ok, but a healthy way to share what you're feeling.

After a death – especially the death of a parent – there can be a dramatic shift in holiday traditions. Instead of packing up the kids to go to mom & dad's house, you might be cooking your first Christmas dinner! You'll have a few rough years to get through before there's a "new normal," but that day will come.

After A Divorce

Divorce can cause a similar grief to losing someone to death. I remember the first Christmas after my ex husband and I separated. The kids were with him on Christmas Eve, and for the first time I was alone. Thank god for my sister! It was one of the most difficult holidays I have spent... and I can't begin to imagine how tough it was on the kids.

Here are some things that you can do after a divorce to help ease the transition for everyone.

1. Be Flexible. Just when you think that you have a solid plan that will work out perfectly, something will inevitably come up. Make sure that you are willing and able to compromise and avoid fighting with your ex, especially in front of the kids.

2. Have reasonable expectations. If you expect to have a Christmas that is like a storybook, you'll need a reality check. The holidays are a very special time of year, but they are never perfect. Cherish every wonderful moment that you have & when difficulties arise, acknowledge them, deal with them, and then let them go.

3. Keep your kids in the loop. Mark on a calendar when they will be with you and when they will be with their other parent. It helps kids feel more secure when they know exactly what the plan is. Don't schedule every minute of their time, though. They will want to have free time to spend with their friends while they are on break from school!

4. Encourage extended family to focus on the children. Studies show that kids do well when they know that they have adults besides their parents who care about them.

5. Buy a gift for the other parent from the kids. This is a tough one, but the children may feel self-conscious if they don't have a gift. Alternately, help them make something that they can give.

Seasons change, people change, lives change and traditions change too. There may be a few difficult years, but you can be confident that things will get better! You'll get your holiday groove back!

 After a divorce, change things up! Don't revisit the same old places. Create new traditions to help you move on.

Meanwhile, change thing up! Don't revisit the same places that you used to go as a couple. Look for new ways to celebrate that won't remind you of the relationship. If you've always cooked a ham, get a turkey! Bake a different dessert this year.

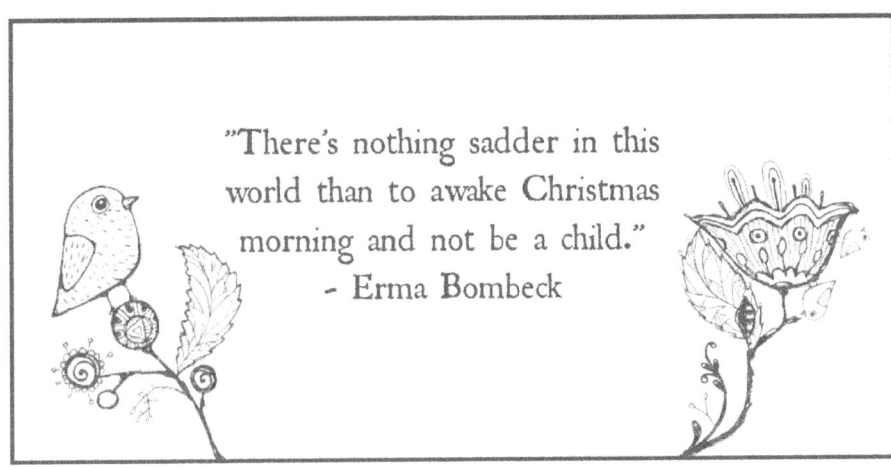

"There's nothing sadder in this world than to awake Christmas morning and not be a child."
- Erma Bombeck

Chapter 6

Spending the Holidays Alone

When you're alone during the holiday season, it can be one of the most difficult times of the year. Everywhere you look there are images of what a "magical" Christmas looks like, & none of them look anything like how you'll be spending the holidays this year!

How do you cope when – for whatever reason - you're not with your family for Christmas? How can you create a season for yourself that has special meaning and brings you joy?

Things to Do

Don't go through the holiday season sitting at home feeling sorry for yourself. Don't volunteer for extra shifts at work. (even though everyone there thinks that you SHOULD so that others can have the time off with their family) You don't have to do that! You still get to celebrate Christmas, so get out, go somewhere, do something!

Visit a local museum. Most are open during the holidays and you'll have fewer crowds to deal with than you might any other time of year.

Check out holiday festivals. There are, of course, parades and celebrations for Christmas, but our local park services offers a winter solstice celebration in the parks with bonfires, hot cider and storytelling. Keep an open mind and full calendar!

Treat yourself! Use the money that you would have used on a gift for a significant other or on family members to treat yourself. Check out a play at the theatre, a hot movie at the theater, or a great new book. How about a luxurious day at the spa? Or an at home spa day, complete with a mani/pedi, facial, and an afternoon nap. Take a candlelight bath, curl up on the couch with a cup of hot tea, a blanket and a movie.

Use the money that you would spend on a nice gift for a significant other and splurge on something for yourself!

Take on a project. Redecorate your bedroom, fix up your bathroom, or rearrange your furniture. Start an indoor garden. Tackle that hall closet and install organizers!

Learn something new. Rediscover an old talent, or learn a new one. Pick up that paint brush again. Take online lessons on fashion design, how to play the guitar, or learn a foreign language! The opportunities are endless and the online classes are usually quite inexpensive.

Get some PUPPY LOVE! It may sound strange, but offering to pet sit for friends gives you an instant four-legged friends for the holidays. What's better than some unconditional love and kisses for Christmas?

Pet sitting for a friend is a great way to get your puppy fix without the long term commitment of pet ownership.

Finding Your Family

When your alone time is getting old, whether you spent two days or two weeks by yourself, move on to some holiday activities that you can do with others.

Volunteer. Volunteer to help out at a shelter or a non-profit organization. Anywhere that there are like minded people. Not only will you be with great people, but volunteering is good for the soul. Pick something that's meaningful to you and you'll feel great!

Throw a Party! Why not host a gathering at your house? Many singles host an annual "orphan's Christmas" celebration each year, inviting old friends and new ones to join them and creating a new "family." Don't assume that your friends have plans throughout the holiday season. Even if they have family commitments, they may still welcome the opportunity to escape for a while and spend time with you.

Host a non-traditional dinner party for your friends. How about a potluck Greek feast or a Moroccan dinner party, complete with a belly dancing competition!

Host a non-traditional holiday gathering. How about a Moroccan dinner party with a belly dancing competition?

How about inviting just a small group of friends over to watch movies or binge watch a TV series that you missed. "Breaking Bad" marathon anyone?

Maybe hosting isn't your style but you don't want to spend Christmas alone. Be honest with friends who ask you if you have plans for the holidays. They may have an extra spot at their table, or have plans to go sledding in the afternoon and invite you to join them.

Getting Away From It All

Maybe the thought of Christmas alone this year is just too much. If you have time off work & nowhere to go, consider booking a vacation. Vacations over the Christmas holiday are becoming more and more popular as people try to escape the holiday mayhem.

Travel & Leisure recently published a list of the best places to spend Christmas, including New Zealand and Brazil. Perhaps you'd prefer paddling in an outrigger canoe with Santa in Hawaii, or relaxing in the snow white sand on a beach in the Dominican Republic.

If you love Christmas, consider Salzburg, Austria. You'll feel like you're walking in a Christmas card! For a spiritual experience, visit Rome, Italy and rent a room in a private house. You may be asked to join in the family's festivities, but if not, there is plenty to do and see.

Check online for special travel packages over the holidays. You can find great deals to any destination you'd like!

Closer to home, you might visit Vermont during the weekend-long Wassail Celebration for caroling, ornament-making workshops and a parade of horse-drawn carriages.

How about window shopping in New York City at Tiffany, Saks Fifth Avenue, Bergdorf Goodman, and Barney's followed with skating at Rockefeller Center?

Do you like to ski? What better time to hit the slopes in Aspen or Vail! Even here in the mid-west there are small ski resorts where you could cozy up, ski to your hearts content, and have a great holiday!

Find Meaning

If you're looking to create a more meaningful Christmas for yourself, there are things that you can do to make the season special for yourself and for others, too!

Adopt an Elderly Person. Wrap up some small gifts and take them to a nursing home in your neighborhood. You can ask staff and they'll tell you - many of the elderly people in care centers don't receive any gifts at Christmas! What kind of gifts are appropriate?

1. Word search puzzle books

2. A box of envelopes and some stamps

3. Warm socks or slippers.

4. A cozy throw blanket.

5. Flowers or plants to brighten up their room.

6. A basket of inexpensive lotions, powder, and other grooming products.

When asked, the majority of nursing home residents will say that the thing they want most is FRESH FRUIT!

All are inexpensive gifts that would make the day of a new elderly friend! You can choose to be totally anonymous if you'd like, or sit and chat with them for a while!

Adopt a Family. If you're not involved with a religious

organization, many hospice centers can connect you with a family that you can adopt. You can go all out and buy gifts, food, and new clothes for them, or keep it simple and give a gift card to a local grocery store or shopping center.

 No one else is responsible for making your days merry and bright, whether you're single or not.

No one else is responsible for making your days merry and bright, whether you're single or not. Truly, there are a lot of positions that you could be in that are worse than being "on your own," so get into the spirit of the seasons and celebrate!

Twelve Days of Good Deeds

Instead of celebrating the Twelve Days of Christmas, celebrate the Twelve Days of Good Deeds! Doing random acts of kindness will help you feel the spirit of the season and will help spread good holiday vibes all across your world!

Donate your old books to the library.

Hold the door for someone.

Deliver homemade cookies to a neighbor.

Leave a treat in your mailbox for the mail carrier.

Hide a few bills in the toy department at the Dollar Store.

Let someone go ahead of you in a checkout line.

Leave quarters in the machines at the laundromat.

Pay for the person behind you in the drive-thru.

Pick up trash someone else dropped.

Shovel your neighbor's sidewalk.

Overtip your waiter or waitress.

Compliment a stranger.

LEAVE QUARTERS IN THE VENDING MACHINE.

DONATE A BAG OF GROCERIES TO THE FOOD SHELF.

Buy lunch for a co-worker.

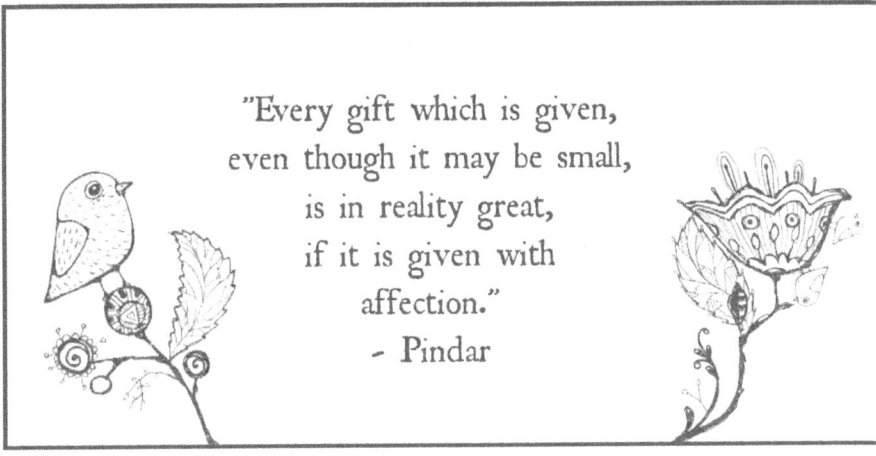

> "Every gift which is given,
> even though it may be small,
> is in reality great,
> if it is given with
> affection."
> - Pindar

Chapter 7
Gifts, Gifting, & Being Gifted

I love giving gifts. I really love it! It brings me so much joy to see the surprised look on someone's face when they open a gift from me and see something that they love.

I work hard all year on holiday gift giving. No, I don't start Christmas shopping in July... but I do pay attention to things that people say throughout the year. Because I have a terrible memory, I have a secret board on Pinterest where I pin all of the gift ideas that I have for my friends and family. As the holidays get closer, I start watching for special deals on those items so that I can get the most bang for my buck.

Gift Solutions for All (Not Gift Cards)

The key to giving the perfect gift is to think of something that you know the receiver will love, but they would never buy themselves. Sometimes you have to spend a bit of money to get something really special, but there are some tricks to getting a perfect gift without breaking the bank.

 Try to avoid giving gift cards. They really send the message that you didn't even make an effort!

Start by making your list early. Like now. I am a huge fan of the website etsy.com for scoring handmade and vintage items that are one of a kind. Keep in mind that these are artists and collectors that are selling – not corporations – so allow plenty of time for them to ship the item to you. Many of the coolest products come from artists in Brazil and other countries and shipping can take several weeks.

eBay is another place to score those one of a kind items. Amazon.com is so awesome for last minute gifts; especially if you're a member of Amazon Prime. You can't beat that free 2 day delivery option!

Try to support local stores when you can. Although I do the majority of my shopping online, I make a special point each year to stop into a local florists shop and support them by purchasing a few gifts.

Last but not least, I've tried to include a few homemade gift ideas in each category for those who may be feeling extra creative and/or cutting back on spending this year. Some of the suggestions are incredibly easy and inexpensive!

You can find tons of ideas for really cool gifts that you can make without too much hassle on Pinterest. If you go to www.pinterest.com/LittleXMas/ you can check out my board of handmade Christmas gift ideas.

Colleagues and Co-workers:

Co-workers can be very difficult to shop for. You want to give a small gift, but it's always a slippery slope and difficult to know. Is it proper to buy a gift for your boss? Your assistant?

Some companies frown on gifts for the boss. If you're new, or not sure what to do, it's always best to ask someone what others have done in the past.

 Gift giving at work is always touchy. If you're not familiar with company policy, but sure that you ask!

Always keep gifts for the boss priced under $50, and make sure that your gift isn't too personal or too lavish. An inspirational book for professionals is always a nice gift, as is a deluxe pen. Consider a group gift where everyone in the office pitches in a small amount of money for a beautiful leather briefcase, travel bag, or a plant for their office.

Here are a few helpful tips on shopping for co-workers:

- Shop early on websites like etsy.com or eBay to score fun, unique, one of a kind or vintage items.

- Stay away from gifts that are too personal, like jewelry, perfume, or bath and body products.

- Gifts of alcohol may be considered inappropriate for the office, depending on the culture.

- Keep it simple. Don't make anyone in the office uncomfortable by purchasing anything too lavish. Stick to an appropriate price range and if you aren't sure, don't be afraid to ask your manager or someone in human resources.

- Think outside the box. A vintage wooden recipe box can hold post-its and pens!

- Consider one large gift that the entire office can enjoy. How about a smoothie maker in the break room with a supply of fresh fruit?

Under $10 Gift Ideas for Co-Workers:

Buy a set of designer office supply items and split it up into several small gifts.

Wrap up a mug from the local coffee shop that they frequent or order a personalized cup cozy.

There are loads of art printables on etsy.com that you could pop into an inexpensive frame.

For the one who packs lunch every day, a cute microwave safe bowl & plate.

Pretty mousepads are inexpensive & fun. Much better than the ones from the supply closet.

Hand sanitizer and lotion for their desk.

A personalized key chain.

For the one who wears heels every day, a soft pair of slipper socks for under her desk.

A leather bound blank book/journal.

Pretty paperclips & note paper.

Under $25 Gift Ideas for Co-Workers:

An air plant in a super cool planter.

A desktop phone or tablet stand.

Travel accessories for the road warrior.

Framed inspirational quotes for the wall.

A nice fountain pen and ink.

Business card holder.

An old fashioned, mounted pencil sharpener.

Holder for reading glasses.

Vintage baskets for in/out.

Nature or art calendar.

Vintage desk accessories.

Business/inspirational book.

Small puzzles and games for their desk.

A desktop lamp or light.

Homemade Gift Ideas for Co-Workers:

Chalkboard Memo Board

1. Find a cool frame at a thrift store and spray paint it in a color that your coworker will love.

2. Using a small pot of chalkboard paint, cover the insert back (where your photo would go) with several coats, allowing to dry thoroughly in between coats.

3. When it's completely dry, wrap 5 or 6 large rubber bands around the back, then insert it into the frame.

Voila! You have made a chalkboard-slash-memo-board that is one of a kind! I've seen many variations of this using everything from chicken wire with little clips for the backing, to twine and clothesline pins for the rubber bands, to using magnetic paint instead of chalkboard paint and giving with cute magnets. Get creative and have fun with it!

Homemade Gift Ideas for Co-Workers:

Covered Footrest

Those plastic footrests that go under your desk? They are absolutely hideous, but they do help your back when you sit at a desk all day.

1. Purchase a plastic footrest at an office supply store. (usually they are under $20)

2. Find a sturdy piece of fabric or a small rug. I used a rag rug from the home improvement store that cost just $1.99.

3. Cut your fabric or rug about 6" larger than the footrest all around.

4. Using two sided carpet tape, attach the fabric to the top and sides of the footrest.

5. Use decorative duck tape to finish the underside edge and to keep the fabric/rug from unraveling.

You have just made a soft, beautiful, custom footrest for under $25!

Gifts for Women

I always think that women are super easy to buy gifts for, but I guarantee that men all over this world disagree with me! Most women that I know are thrilled with any small luxury item.

An easy idea is to look at the things she already has and uses regularly and step it up a bit. If the woman in your life uses hand lotion several times a day, indulge her with some luxury hand cream. If you know that she loves chocolate, find some fine European chocolates to spoil her with.

 Need gift ideas? Look at the recipient's Pinterest boards - especially if there's one called "WISH LIST" - for easy answers!

You may spend a bit more money on these items, but to me, the whole idea of gifting is to give something special that they would never buy for themselves.

Here are a few helpful tips on shopping for the ladies in your life:

- When it comes to clothing, don't guess on the size. Do some homework before hand. If you truly don't know, find a store clerk for help... preferably one who appears to be about the same size as the woman you are shopping for.

- It is absolutely never okay to give any sort of cleaning supplies. No vacuum, iron, etc. No way.

- Make sure it's appropriate. Don't give a teenage babysitter a massage gift certificate, or alcohol to a teacher. It might be OK in your situation, but it may cause problems. Better to be safe!

- When in doubt, don't fall back on a gift card. Take time to select something that you think she'll love. Include a gift receipt and a note to say she can exchange it for something else. At least she'll know that you made an effort.

Under $25 Gifts for Women:

A set of fun, colorful bracelets.

A blank journal with a nice pen.

Scented candles.

A wired handset for her cell phone.

Fizzy luxury bath bombs from LUSH.

A fun coin purse or wallet.

Fine European chocolates.

A rollerball version of her favorite perfume.

A set of nice makeup brushes.

MAC lipstick, Chanel nail polish, or any small item with a very luxurious brand name.

A tea infuser and cute mug.

A telephoto lens and tripod for her cell phone.

Under $50 Gifts for Women:

Gloves that you can use with touchscreens.

A designer iPhone case.

Soft, warm slippers.

A silk scarf or pashmina.

Stackable rings.

Penguin Classics hardcover books.

Luxury herbal bath products.

A Diptyque mini candle.

An organic skincare set..

A nice, classic tote bag from Lands End.

Fun and funky rain boots.

Luxury Gifts for Women:

A tablet or e-reader with a gift card for books.

A classic leather motorcycle jacket.

A cashmere throw blanket.

Soft bathrobe and pajamas with a spa gift certificate.

Lounge clothes; knit pants and a hoodie for hanging out.

A fitbit activity tracker if she works out.

New UGGS.

A Clairsonic Skin Care brush.

Her favorite designer handbags latest style.

Gifts for Men

The men in my life have always been easy to buy gifts for because they need everything! They seldom buy clothes, shoes, toiletries, etc. for themselves, so picking out a little nicer version of what I typically would select for them is one easy way to gift them over the holidays.

But sometimes you want to give just a little more... something special to show how much you care. Here are a few ideas for those situations.

Under $25 Gifts for Men:

Ticket stub diary.

Leather key fob.

Portable emergency phone charger.

A nice leather wallet from Marshalls or TJMaxx.

Beard conditioning oil or shaving soap.

Vintage comic books with covers scanned & framed.

Power adapter decals for his phone charger.

Wooden iPhone or iPad case.

Dopp kit toiletry bag.

Superman socks!

Under $50 Gifts for Men:

Golf balls with a gift certificate to the indoor driving range.

Leather mouse pad.

Cufflinks.

Wool blanket from the Swiss Army surplus store.

Lordship! For $29.99 you can purchase 1 sq. ft. of land in Scotland from "Highland Titles".

Men's organic skincare products.

Vintage concert t-shirts.

A new polar fleece jacket to layer for winter.

Nice wool dress socks from SmartWool.

A designer tie from one of his favorite designers.

Luxury Gifts for Men:

A telescope and a book on stargazing.

A subscription to NextIssue for a year. Just $14.99 a month to access hundreds of magazines on your tablet.

A guitar with lessons on how to play.

Vintage sports memorabilia.

Tickets to an upcoming concert or hockey game.

Shearling slippers by Ugg.

A solar cell phone charger.

Heated ice scraper for his car.

His favorite cologne with some lotion for men. They get dry skin too!

When You're Cutting Back

Sometimes we just can't afford to do everything we want to for everyone we want to at Christmas time. Or perhaps there are other reasons you've decided to scale things back a bit and simplify your gift giving this year.

I'll admit that gift giving gets to be a lot to juggle – even with just my two boys! I've always tried to not only keep the number of packages the same, but also the dollar amount spent on each of them the same. It's only fair, after all! I keep a spreadsheet to make it easier on myself, but I'm thinking that maybe this year even that will go away.

The four gift rule:
"Something you want, something you need, something to wear, something to read."

I have seen "the rule of four" online before as a gift giving guideline that many families use. It goes something like this..."Something you want, something you need, something to wear, something to read." It doesn't go into details about how much money is spent on each item or on each person, but each family member receives a total of 4 gifts. It's a pretty great concept and worth considering...though sometimes limitations and rules can make things more difficult overall.

One of the most important things that you can do when you decide to make significant changes in your giving is to communicate! If you have friends and family that you typically exchange gifts with, drop them a quick note and explain to them that, for whatever reason, you're not going to do gifts this year (or you're only going to do handmade gifts, or baked goods, or whatever).

Communication is especially important when young children are involved. If your kids are used to receiving a pile of gifts on Christmas morning and they wake up instead to one package under the tree, it will be difficult for them even with advance warning. It's only fair to give them a heads-up.

With adult friends and family - letting them know of your situation in advance allows them to decide for themselves if they want to do a similar gift for you, or stick with their usual plan.

If you're cutting back on giving, for whatever reason, letting people know in advance will help make things less awkward.

When you do meet over the holidays, if they give you a nice gift after you've already told them that you're cutting back, know that you communicated your situation to them and they gifted you because they wanted to. Perhaps they had a high income year and wanted to splurge a bit. Perhaps they found an item for you that they really wanted you to have and it brings them joy to give you. For whatever reason, accept the gift politely and say thank you.

Learning to Receive

I learned how to "receive" from my mom. We have this thing in our family...nobody can give anyone anything without having that person:

> A. Decline to take it.

> B. Immediately find something to give you.

> C. Try to pay you for the item.

Finally, when my mom reached a certain age, I think she got tired of hearing it. When someone would protest a gift of any sort, saying something like, "Oh you shouldn't have!" or "I can't accept that" mom would say "Just shut up and say thank you."

 When someone gives you a beautiful gift, just say "Thank You."

Guess what. It worked! At least most of the time, family members started just saying "thank you" and receiving the gift.

Why does receiving a gift make us feel so uncomfortable? Is it because we don't feel worthy of the gift?

Sometimes, I think it just makes us squirm if we don't have a gift to give in return. If that is the case for you, please refer to the very sentence of the first page of this chapter. It brings me so much joy to give someone a small gift – just a token of my appreciation – that I never have considered that it might make the receiver uncomfortable. Then again, I have been on the receiving end of gifts that I've not reciprocated. I have a very generous neighbor who leaves a gift on our doorstep each year at Christmastime and I have never once done anything other than thank him.

This holiday season, when you receive a beautiful gift from someone, don't say "You shouldn't have!" Don't worry if you don't have a gift for them. And for God's sake, don't feel unworthy. Listen to my mom and "Just shut up and say thank you."

"Maybe Christmas, he thought,
doesn't come from a store.
Maybe Christmas, perhaps,
means a little bit more!"
- Dr. Suess

Chapter 8
Finding Meaning in the Holidays

Some argue that Christmas is a cultural holiday these days as opposed to a religious holiday. This, of course, doesn't mean that there are no religious aspects to a Christmas celebration, because there certainly are! Religion is an important part of any culture and an important part of the Christmas tradition.

Culture, though, is more than just religion, which means that it is possible that Christmas has become something more than a religious holiday, even though it is a day that has been set aside to celebrate the birth of Jesus Christ.

In the small town where I grew up, our family attended mass every year on Christmas eve at the local Catholic church. I remember that it was one of the few times each year when the church was packed, and I wondered where all of the people came from. I remember that the mass was exceptionally long, and that I could barely keep my eyes open. But I didn't dare fall asleep. I remember that the church was beautifully decorated with bright red poinsettia plants. And I remember that I couldn't wait to get home to see if Santa had come while we were at church.

Celebrating When You're Not Religious

These days, we don't go to midnight mass, but we celebrate in different ways. No one celebrates Christmas the same way, and no one celebrates every possible aspect of Christmas. Some hang mistletoe, some don't; some drink eggnog, some don't; some have a creche, some don't.

Everyone celebrates the holidays differently, and it's just that kind of diversity that makes things interesting!

Everyone has traditions that are more meaningful than others, and most create some of their own "traditions." The result is that everyone chooses certain aspects of Christmas to celebrate.

If you want to celebrate Christmas with your family in your own way, there is no reason why you shouldn't. Celebrate the traditions that are meaningful to you, including the Christian traditions if you wish.

Other Holiday Traditions

Maybe your family celebrates Hanukah or Kwanza. Maybe your family celebrates a little bit of Christmas, Hanukah and Kwanza.

I think that knowing about others traditions and perhaps implementing a bit of each into your holiday season is a beautiful thing. If it's meaningful to you, then you should do it. Your family will grow up in this world better aware of other traditions and celebrations.

The holidays aren't just for Christians or Jews or African-Americans or people who believe in something. Really, the holidays aren't about presents or Santa Claus. They aren't really meant only for children (as some believe), but they are for all of us. The holidays aren't about the obligatory family visits and having to sit through dinner with people you don't really know or like.

The holidays aren't just for Christians or Jews or African-Americans or people who believe in something.

They aren't about stuffing ourselves, watching football, or "getting away from it all." They aren't about decorating your home in just the right way, having 5 Christmas trees or stringing up thousands of lights on the outside of your house.

The holidays and Christmas are time to take a good look at your life. They are about finding something special and beautiful about yourself, your life, and the people who make it special.

They are about recognizing the small, beautiful things in your life and appreciating them.

They are about looking at our crazy lives that are full of ups and downs and being grateful that we are alive. We have people that we love and that love us.

No matter what you believe, we all know that the holiday season is about something special... something that is bigger than us. We can feel it! It's the celebrating and all of the pressure that we put on ourselves this time of year that make us lose touch of the things that are the most important to us.

We get so caught up in the decorating, the entertaining, the clothes, the gifts and all of the ribbons and bows that we forget the whole point of the season.

 We get so caught up in the decorating, the entertaining, the clothes, the gifts and all of the ribbons and bows that we forget the whole point of the season.

Really, why get excited about Christmas if you don't allow yourself time to do the things that are meaningful for you? Why bother with obligations if you go through with them because you feel like you have no choice?

You always have a choice. Remember, you get to pick! If you don't want to go to spend Christmas with your family this year, you can choose to do something different. It doesn't mean that you don't love your family or that they aren't important to you. It just means that you want to celebrate Christmas in a way that brings you more joy and helps bring more meaning to this time of year for you and your family.

There's no real secret to "Creating A Beautiful Little Christmas" that we don't all know already. The decisions that you make every single day help create the life that you live. During the holidays, the decisions that you make help create the Christmas that you celebrate.

It's being aware of the things that you value and don't value, then choosing to expend your energy in the areas that will mean the most to you and your family - THAT is how you create a beautiful Christmas! It's the love and energy that you share with those around you that make the season special. It's the small gestures that can make a difference in the lives of our friends and family.

Life is too short and too beautiful – the holiday season especially – to spend your days dreading any part of it! When you choose to make your life beautiful and make your Christmas beautiful, you are celebrating in the very best possible way.

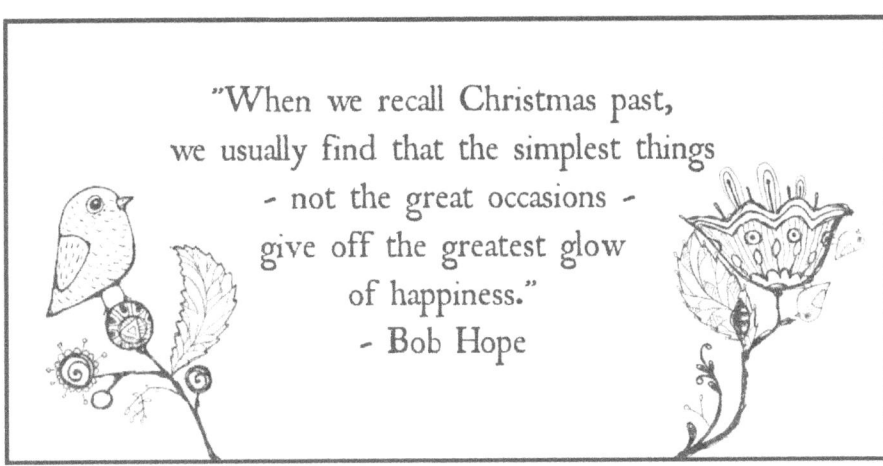

"When we recall Christmas past,
we usually find that the simplest things
- not the great occasions -
give off the greatest glow
of happiness."
- Bob Hope

Chapter 9
Self-Care

Taking care of yourself during the holiday season is one of the best gifts you can give to yourself and your family. When you take good care of your needs, you are much better prepared to take care of others. Taking steps to simplify your holidays is a good first step towards creating a beautiful little Christmas, but nothing will impact your holiday season like practicing good self care.

Self care is a foreign concept to many women who are used to carrying the load for their entire household. You need to know that it is not selfish to take care of your needs. You can't go nonstop over the holidays without making sure that your needs are being met.

Some needs are very basic, like making sure that you get enough sleep, you eat right, and you get some exercise each day. Some needs are a bit more complicated. Making sure that you are trusting your instincts, being kind to yourself, saying what you mean; those things are sometimes more difficult, but no less important.

 Making sure that you are trusting your instincts, being kind to yourself, and saying what you mean. It's the best form of self care.

Letting Go

One of the most important elements of practicing good self care is letting go of the things that are out of your control. Thinking too much about situations that you have no control over is a huge cause of stress. This type of thinking makes you feel powerless, causes anxiety and feelings of hopelessness.

When you catch yourself worrying about something that you can't control, consciously make a switch and focus on something that you CAN DO to make your immediate situation better. If you're worried about your family gathering for the holidays, focus instead on the food prep for the dinner that you'll serve. If you're worried about whether or not people will like and appreciate the gifts that you bought for them, shift your focus to wrapping them beautifully so that they look beautiful under the tree.

Maybe you find yourself living in the past during the holiday season. It's great to look back on happy holiday memories, but if you find yourself continually focusing on difficult past incidents or regrets, you'll definitely want to nip that in the bud! Ask yourself why you are still holding on to that moment. Try to figure out what exactly happened and why it continues to upset you. Once you have the facts around what actually happened, figure out what you were meant to learn from the experience and use that to your benefit. When you catch yourself thinking about the situation, remind yourself of the lesson that you discovered and move forward.

 During the holidays, we are incredibly hard on ourselves. It's easy to start listening to negative self-talk. DON'T BELIEVE IT FOR A MINUTE!

During the holidays, we are incredibly hard on ourselves. It's easy to start listening to negative self-talk. A lot of that comes from past holidays, memories and relationships.

You might be thinking, like so many of us do, that you're not a very good cook so you could NEVER entertain during the holidays. You might think that it doesn't matter what you wear because you're fat. It won't look good anyhow. You might think that you're not a creative person and you don't have time to try to make homemade gifts. DON'T BELIEVE IT!

You don't have to be a professional chef to host a holiday gathering. There are recipes in this book that you can put together very easily and will be delicious!

None of us are model-thin beauties, but we make the best of what we've got because when we look pretty, we feel better. When we feel better about ourselves, we spread joy to the people around us.

As for crafting and decorating, some people are into it and some people aren't. The fact that you don't think you'd be good at it is no reason to walk away from your creativity! It's a beautiful way to express yourself and give a gift that truly comes from the heart. Even the most creative artists abandon projects halfway through and start over. The only difference is that they keep trying until they get something that they love!

 When you let go of the hang-ups and the "I cant's" you free yourself to be the person who really CAN create a beautiful Christmas!

When you let go of the hang-ups and the "I cant's" you free yourself to be the person who really CAN create a beautiful Christmas – and a beautiful life.

Expecting perfection during the holidays is a surefire way to set yourself up for disappointment. One of the best ways that you can take care of yourself is to accept that things will go wrong, and be prepared to deal with it when it happens! Christmas dinner may not turn out the way you wanted it to, the kids might have a meltdown – heck, YOU might have a meltdown! Preparing yourself for things to go wrong can be a great way to take care of yourself!

When it comes to something big, like your holiday dinner, you might want to have a back up plan of some sort. Even if that plan is that you have the phone number to the Chinese restaurant that delivers on speed dial at least you know that you have an alternative if things go south.

Asking for Help

Holiday parties, family gatherings, and other holiday activities are all fun, but the extra demands on our time and attention can be a big cause of holiday stress. When you add in some travel, meal preparation, shopping and having guests at the house you could be setting yourself up for an extra stressful season.

If you're feeling overwhelmed at the thought of having to cook an entire holiday dinner, ask family members to help either by bringing a dish to share or by coming to your home early to help prepare the meal.

Sometimes getting the house ready is the thing that is the most difficult. Cleaning, getting rooms ready for guests, keeping up with laundry and dishes is a lot of work. Is there a neighborhood teen that you could hire to come in and help you with some of the housework? Is there a family member that's creative and would like to come in and help you with some of the decorating? Can you afford to hire a maid service come in and do a deep cleaning? Whatever it takes to get things done, don't try to do it all by yourself!

Pamper, Pamper, Pamper!

Make sure that you don't forget to take some time for yourself. Stopping at the salon for a mani/pedi can make you feel like a new woman! Here's a list of ideas on how you can pamper yourself during the busy holiday season.

1. Take a relaxing bath with a candle burning and the lights dimmed.

2. Stop into the salon for a mani/pedi while you're out shopping.

3. Make a cup of tea and watch cat videos on YouTube.

4. Order yourself a sexy new bra and panties set online.

5. Pour a glass of wine and pop in the movie "Love Actually".

6. Dish yourself a bowl of ice cream and catch up on your reality TV shows.

7. Take a walk outside in nature.

8. Go for a drive at night and look at the homes that are all lit up in your neighborhood.

9. Have coffee at a local coffee shop while you read a book.

10. A 30 minute massage is wonderful, but a 60 minute massage is even better!

11. Give yourself a facial at home.

12. Do a long yoga workout.

13. Buy a single slice of chocolate cake and enjoy every bite by yourself!

14. Go to bed extra early one night or sleep late one morning. Take a nap.

15. Write in your diary or journal.

16. Browse through a bookstore while you're out shopping and find yourself a new book or magazine.

17. Go see a movie in the theater all by yourself.

18. Pop in your favorite CD and dance around the kitchen while you're cooking.

19. Buy yourself flowers or a new potted plant.

When You Can't Take Any More!

That meltdown that I mentioned earlier? Well, sometimes that kind of thing happens during the holidays. Go to your room, hang a "do not disturb" sign on your door and cry it out. This is a tough time of year for many people, yet the expectation is that everyone should be happy and get along. Get real.

Keep a comfort kit handy. It's a small tote bag that you keep nearby that contains special items that you associate with being comforted.

When you feel like you can't take it anymore, it's great to have a "comfort kit" ready to go so that you can give yourself some immediate pampering.

What is a comfort kit? It's a small tote bag that you keep nearby that contains special items that you associate with being comforted. I recommend that everyone have one readily available all the time!

When you're stressed out and on the verge of a meltdown it's impossible to know what you need to make yourself feel better. Having a little goody bag tucked in your closet can be a lifesaver. What should you put in your comfort kit?

- a scented candle

- lip balm

- aromatherapy essential oils

- some luxury hand cream

- a soft, cashmere wrap

- Rescue Remedy spray

- chocolates

- wine

- a journal and a pretty pen

- soft, furry socks

- a puzzle book like Sudoku

- an inspirational book

How fabulous does that sound? It kind of makes you want to have a meltdown so that you can go in your room and dig in to your comfort kit, right?

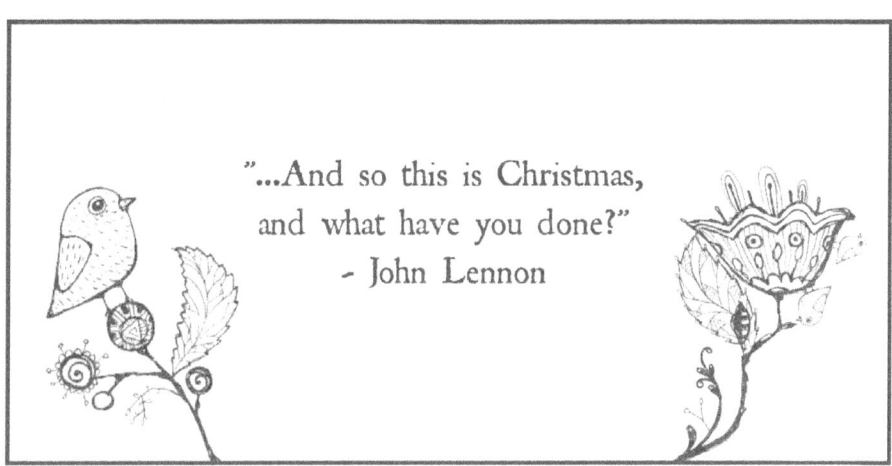

"...And so this is Christmas,
and what have you done?"
- John Lennon

Chapter 10

Your Worst Holiday Problems

After sending a quick poll out to friends and family, I was inundated with questions on how to handle some really difficult holidays situations. Here are a few of the best questions and a few suggestions on how you might handle the situation if you are in a similar predicament.

"What do you do when you are hosting extended family for the holidays and while your family enjoys a cocktail, your in-laws cringe at the sight of a wine bottle?"

I think that your family can have a drink or two and can still be respectful of your in-laws. Be discreet, but don't try to hide the fact that there is alcohol being served. You won't be fooling anyone.

I would recommend that you make a ginger simple syrup and use it as a base for all of your beverages.

Ginger Simple Syrup

4 cups water
a small piece of fresh ginger,
sliced into coins
2 cups of sugar

In a small saucepan, stir to
combine and bring to a boil.
Continue to heat on a simmer for
about 20 minutes.

Strain and transfer to a glass
container and allow to cool to room
temperature.

One of my favorite winter cocktails is Jameson Irish Whiskey and Gingerale. To make it, you'd add 1-1/2 oz. Jameson, 2 oz. ginger syrup, and sparkling water. I love it with a sprinkle of sugar and a piece of fresh ginger.

To make a ginger martini, combine 2 oz. of vodka, 2 ounces ginger syrup, a dash of lemon juice, and a small sprig of fresh mint. Shake over ice and serve chilled.

For those who don't drink, you can use the same ginger syrup mixed with soda water, a bit of lemon juice and mint to make a delicious homemade ginger ale. If you'd like, you could also add a little grenadine and a cherry for a bit of festive cheer.

By providing a similar beverage both with and without alcohol, you eliminate some of the discomfort associated with serving alcohol at a family gathering.

"We are celebrating the holidays at a ski resort and our young children will be expecting Santa to come. We can't wrap gifts before we leave home because of airport security, and our bag space is limited. What should we do?"

You didn't mention what your budget is like, but I did a quick online search for "small electronic games for kids" and hit the jackpot! There are tablets for all ages that are educational and entertaining!

Nintendo Wii or DS are good options both for younger and older kids. They have early childhood games and games for everyone!

Another option is to order your gifts online and have them shipped directly to the resort. Contact them first to make sure that it's OK, but stores like amazon.com will even gift wrap items before they ship them. That way, when you arrived at your destination your gifts would be waiting for you!

"What should I do if an acquaintance drops by unexpectedly with a gift for me, and I don't have a gift for them?"

First of all, you are lucky to have friends that care enough about you to want to give you a gift, so count your blessings and thank them for their friendship, not just at Christmastime but all year long.

If you are really uncomfortable with the thought of being caught empty handed, you can certainly wrap up a few extra gifts to keep under the tree for a situation just like this. An inexpensive pashmina scarf, an aromatherapy scented candle, a nice bottle of body lotion – all would make great gifts that you could give anyone and they would be thrilled!

"I'm invited to several potluck gatherings over the holidays and I'm worried about bringing a dish that will be okay sitting out for a couple of hours. I don't want anyone getting sick from my food! Is there a go-to dish that would be a good choice for me to bring?"

It's smart to plan ahead for a potluck when you're not sure how long the food will sit out without refrigeration. I make a Lemon Quinoa Salad that everyone loves, and because it doesn't have any ingredients that spoil quickly (dairy or meat) it would be a perfect choice for you. Not only that, but it's a really healthy dish that will help balance out all of the rich, heavy food. My recipe serves about 12, so if you have a big crowd you'll want to double the recipe.

Light Lemon Quinoa Salad

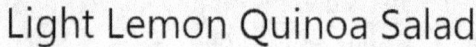

Ingredients for Dressing:
Zest & juice of 1 large lemon
1/3 c olive oil
1 tsp. ground coriander
1 tsp. ground cumin
1 tsp. paprika
Salt & ground black pepper
Ingredients for Salad:
2 c quinoa, rinsed well
1 tsp. salt
4 c cold water
2 c dried cranberries
12 cup diced dried apricots
Warm water
3 avocados
4 green onions, sliced
12 c toasted slivered almonds

Mix lemon zest & juice, olive oil, coriander, cumin & paprika. Season to taste with salt and pepper.

In a saucepan, combine quinoa, salt and cold water; bring to a boil over medium-high heat. Stir, reduce heat to low, cover and simmer for about 15 minutes or until water is absorbed and quinoa is tender. Fluff with a fork, spread on a large baking sheet and let cool completely. Place cranberries and apricots in a bowl. Cover with warm water and let stand for about 5 minutes or until plump. Drain & set aside.

Peel avocados and cut into bite-sized chunks. Toss with 1 Tbsp. of the dressing to prevent discoloration. Place cooled quinoa in a large salad bowl. Add cranberry mixture, avocados, green onions and almonds. Add the remaining dressing and toss to combine.

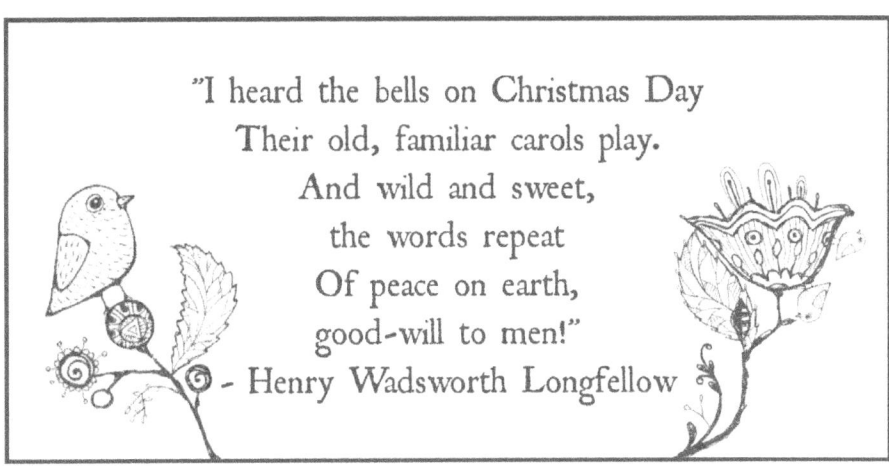

"I heard the bells on Christmas Day
Their old, familiar carols play.
And wild and sweet,
the words repeat
Of peace on earth,
good-will to men!"
- Henry Wadsworth Longfellow

Chapter 11
A Very Merry Christmas

As you enjoy your holidays this season, pay close attention to how you are feeling. If you begin feeling anxious and stressed, practice good self-care and take some time to relax. If things start to get overwhelming, think about how you can either cut back a bit more or request help from a friend or family member.

Change can be difficult for many people, and you might be nervous about your commitment to keeping Christmas simple this year. Friends and family may not even notice a difference, but they may respond negatively. Situations may arise that make you doubt one of the decisions you've made.

It's okay to not have all of the answers. Christmas comes every year, and every year you have a new opportunity to decide how you would like to celebrate the season. Next year you may decide to add a few things back into your schedule that were missed, or you may decide to cut back even more. Don't be surprised if people start asking you for advice on how to scale back a bit themselves.

Know that whatever happens this Christmas, you'll have the tools that you need to make next Christmas even better for you and your family.

Relax and enjoy the beauty and peace around you during this magical time of year.

A Very Merry Christmas to you and yours!

About the Author:

Teri Ahlm is a blogger at abeautifullittlelife.com where she writes about doing small, everyday things with great care to make them special; and how by doing something special every day, you are creating a beautiful little life for yourself and your family.

Teri is a mom of two boys, aged 21 and 17, two dogs and two cats. Teri is married to her best friend and they are living their beautiful little life together in Minneapolis, Minnesota.

www.ingramcontent.com/pod-product-compliance
Lightning Source LLC
Chambersburg PA
CBHW071042290526
45795CB00004B/1271